Reflective Leaders and High-Performance Organizations

How Effective Leaders Balance Task and Relationship to
Build High-Performing Organizations

NICK A. SHEPHERD
AND
PETER J. SMYTH

iUniverse, Inc.
Bloomington

Reflective Leaders and High-Performance Organizations
How Effective Leaders Balance Task and Relationship to Build
High-Performing Organizations

iUniverse books may be ordered through booksellers or by contacting:

iUniverse
1663 Liberty Drive
Bloomington, IN 47403
www.iuniverse.com
1-800-Authors (1-800-288-4677)

ISBN: 978-1-4620-2365-3 (sc)
ISBN: 978-1-4620-7267-5 (hc)
ISBN: 978-1-4620-2366-0 (ebk)

Library of Congress Control Number: 2011962922

Printed in the United States of America

iUniverse rev. date: 02/09/2012

CONTENTS

Acknowledgments ix
Foreword.. xiii

Chapter 1 Introduction...1
    The Changing Business Environment 6
    The Need for a New Paradigm...14

Chapter 2 "Partners in Success":
    Why Task and Relationship? 17

Chapter 3 The Changing Face of "Task"...............................30
    Follow the Money to Reduce Costs....................................39

Chapter 4 Shared Values: Foundation for Relationships.............43
    Building an Organizational Values Framework.............47

Chapter 5 Leadership and a Values-Based Organization.............60
    Leadership and the Integration of Values 60
    Leadership and Narcissism 62
    The Values-Based Leader...65
    Leadership and Dissonance 69
    Leadership and Team Effectiveness 71
    The Team Shamrock 75
    The Underfunctioning Team...77

Chapter 6 Making It Real:

A Relationship-Based Organization 78

Leadership and the Values-Based Organization..............78

The Team as a Challenge for Leadership 79

The Core Model of Team Development............................81

Stage 1: Formation 82

Stage 2: Deliberation 87

Stage 3: Amalgamation 89

Stage 4: Consolidation 90

Stage 5: Summation..92

Stage 6: Evaluation...95

The Leader and the "As-If" Team 97

Leadership and Change 101

Barriers to Effective Communication 110

Chapter 7 Effective Integration of Task and Relationship 113

Planning for Effectiveness 119

Human Dimensions, Leadership, and "People"............. 124

Relationships, Clients, and Customers............................ 131

People and the Process Dimension 137

People and Partners/Suppliers 142

Internal Controls and Task/Relationship 144

Relationships, Results, and Improvements..................... 146

Enhanced Task through Foundational
Relationships—Recap... 148

Chapter 8 Knowing It's Real: Building and
Using Measurements 151

Measuring Leadership Effectiveness................................ 153

Chapter 9 Task and Relationship in Practice: Case Studies...... 157

Case 1 Manufacturing Subsidiary of a
Family Business.. 157

Background to Our Participation................................ 157
Task: Relationship Development............................ 158
Additional Challenges and Learnings 161
Evolution of the Team Development and
Ongoing Benefits 162
Case 2 Resource Industry: Joint Venture........................ 163
Background to Our Participation............................. 163
Task: Relationship Development............................. 164
Steps to Success.. 167
Additional Challenges and Learnings.................... 170
Case 3 Public Sector Leadership Team............................ 171
Case 4 International Pharmaceutical Company:
A European Operation.. 175

Chapter 10 Organizational Theory and Leadership 182
An Evolving History 182
The Behavioral Application of Values in Leadership.... 182
The Use of Psychometric Assessments 190
Call to Action: Summary of Next Steps.......................... 192

Appendices: Examples and Templates.. 197

Background on the Authors.. 199
Examples of Joint Consulting Projects 205
The RP5 Management Model of Excellence.................... 208
ACT Team Assessment 211
ACT Team Assessment 212
Results of ACT Assessment in Practice 213
Example of Survey of Individual and 360-degree
Task/Relationship Assessment............................. 214
Values Evaluation and Assessment................................... 216
Application Note:... 217

Assessment of Commitment to Values by
    Managers during Development............................ 218
Example of a Developing Definition to Understand
    the Stated Value... 219
The GROWS Framework.. 220
The Answer to the Dots 221

Bibliography 223

ACKNOWLEDGMENTS

As every author knows, developing a book is truly a long-term labor of love. It is easy to say, "Let's write a book," and start developing the contents, ideas, charts, and diagrams, but when the initial enthusiasm wanes, we all need that push to move things ahead. We count ourselves lucky that through this process, we have been able to use our complementary patterns of behavior as needed. Peter's exhortations of "So when are we going to get this finished?" combined with Nick's constant promises of "I just have this to finish (or that to change)" seemed to keep us going. As we neared the finish post, the constant updating, amending, and (we hope) improving seemed to take on its own life and start us down the perpetual road of constantly being "almost complete." But here we are, with a finished product. We ask readers' indulgence that this type of writing is always a "work in progress," as is our journey through life.

While the work in developing this book has come from much of our consulting activity together over the last twenty years or more, we have also had the privilege to cross paths with many wonderful people who have contributed to both our thinking and our development. They often challenged us and always added to and enlarged upon what we ourselves had developed. In particular, we would like to recognize the following for their individual contributions to our ongoing learning: Bob White,

Lynda Shephard, Tim Water, Don Walter, Suzanne Court, Michael Court, Philip Court, Doug Major, Dawn Coburn-Joy, Doug Nicholson, Guy Gordon, Howard Steinberg, Rod Barr, Kim Stratton, Tom Stewart, Frank Milligan, David Pike, Stewart Desson, Janice Parviainen, Gisela Neitzert, John Furlan, Gary Burge, Philip McKenna, Neill MacMillan, Alan Maclachlan, and Karen Porter-Lee.

In addition to listing books by several people we actually interact with, the bibliography attempts to focus the reader on just a sampling of the amazing breadth of great works that are out there, which help us try to understand both the human condition as well as the nature of work groups, individuals, and interactions. We live in exciting and amazing times; at a high (mature?) level as the human race, we are at a stage in our development where advances in communications and transportation have brought about globalization, within which we have the opportunity to interact with every other person on the planet. Many visionaries have seen the opportunity to bring people together for better understanding and harmony, such as Sir John A. Macdonald in Canada, the founding fathers of the American constitution, and more recently John Monnet and Robert Schuman, who foresaw the integration of Europe as a way of enhancing the opportunities for peaceful coexistence in the future, instead of fighting wars, which has been the way conflicts have been resolved for centuries.

We believe that this approach must permeate the very institutions where we as humans come together to create, invent, cooperate, and collaborate, whether it is providing public sector services or working in the for-profit sector. The better we understand ourselves and each other, the more likely it is that we will resolve our perceptions and preconditions, which often get in the way of working effectively to achieve common goals. Nowhere is this global evolution better analyzed than through the work of author Jeremy Rifkin; those interested in the broader evolution of the human race toward a framework of maturity and interdependence should read his book *The Empathic Civilization.*

In addition, we are both so thankful to have supportive families that have certainly made many suggestions to our work, but more important than that, they have taught us many of the lessons of life and provided the support that is so necessary and so appreciated in an undertaking such as this. Thank you to the Gawdiak-Smyth clan, Aretta, Aedan, Ciara, Taigh, and to the Shepherds and their extended family: Janet, Sarah, Lee-Jane and Ted, and David and Abbey. In particular, we both appreciate the many, many years of support from our spouses and their patience with our sometimes strange discussions and ideas.

Finally, we need to say thank you to those who gave us the support for that final push for publication, including all of the team that we dealt with at iUniverse. While we had many choices in how to "go to market," the one who clinched the deal was Denise Benefiel, who followed up on our initial interest and provided guidance, help, assurance, and coaching that led to our decision to work with her company.

tools, performance metrics, and quality mechanisms, among others, have perpetuated the notion of an optimization threshold when it comes to task management. In broad terms, Western culture's tenacious bent on maximizing output—in the form of individualized, itemized profit—has imperiled our ability to detect the vast risks this tendency imposes on our relationships within the collectivity. In the twofold process of cultural survival—adapting to an external environment while integrating within the internal group to which we belong—we today tend to place too much emphasis on *adapting externally* (task focus), and less on *integrating* within our clan, our in-group, our immediate team members (relationship focus).

We thus find ourselves uncomfortably requiring continued training in our organizations in order to learn and re-learn what it means to behave as one part of a whole, to build a team and manage our role therein, and to sustain meaningful relationships. We have necessarily built barriers between our private and public personas, and have instinctively sought to protect what is ours, as time and space have become compressed and monetarized commodities. The paradox of this balancing act between task and relationship is that this need to re-center our attention on the relationship emerges in an environment where measuring individualized yield has remained a core focus of business process optimization.

Yet upon examining team values in large organizations, specific differentiating factors point to a form of tacit knowledge, linked to group intelligence, which is very prevalent in traditionally collectivist cultures (India, Asia, Africa, Middle East . . .)—in other words, in the regions where the mass of the world's population is to be found. As the economies in some of these regions reach mature stages of industrialization, the inhabitants continue the inevitable shift towards individualization, greater self-expression, and a newfound independence of choice. We're already witnessing some changes in the way group intelligence is expressed and transmitted in these regions and may ask ourselves if accessing prosperity necessarily forcibly means a weakened group intelligence. The irony of this is that as organizational behavior studies in the West focus on the qualities inherent to the collective (re-vamping relationships), many dominantly collectivist cultures are swinging in the opposite direction, focused on cultural individuation more than ever (moving to greater task orientation).

Embracing this contemporary paradox, *Reflective Leaders and High-Performance Organizations* revisits a question which has been framed in different ways in recent years: How optimal can a team be when its tasks are synchronized but its members are out of sync on the relationship level? Peter and Nick's insights corroborate the broad dissatisfaction that a majority of teams express about their collective effectiveness and the leadership guiding them, and the numbers speak for themselves. Noting that in " . . . a range of teams, from medicine to manufacturing, our research suggests that on a 1–10 scale (10 being high), the average team scores an 8 on Task focus and 3 on Relationship developments," it becomes clear that the imbalance needs correction. Somewhere along the way to optimization, human concerns got temporarily sidelined. Most of us have experienced this firsthand as organizational philosophies shifted from humanistic to technology-centric, which inherently deepened what David Harvey calls "time-space compression" (1999) and the exponential acceleration of information transfer.

Today's economy requires us in the West to "innovate or die" as we participate in the leap from the Information age to what Daniel Pink calls the "Conceptual Age" in his book *A Whole New Mind*. He acknowledges that economic advantage can no longer be derived from the logical, analytical skills of knowledge workers but from creative, conceptual, and relationship skills. As the technicians of the 20th century are supplanted by "artists, inventors, designers, storytellers . . . big picture thinkers," it becomes apparent that organizational design, along with human resource management and strategy, are going to be undergoing several facelifts in the future.

And this is what makes *Reflective Leaders and High-Performance Organizations* such a timely read: it brings us to a fundamental level of human engagement within an organization and attempts to make sense of our role in the task-relationship dyad. Thinking back to Simone de Beauvoir's observation of the precedence of *becoming* over a fixed identity, we are reminded of the dynamic shifts occurring literally as we read these pages, and how closely linked these transformations are to the potential of some good leaders and their organizations to become truly great.

Michelle Mielly, Ph.D.
Grenoble Graduate School of Business
November 2011

CHAPTER 1

INTRODUCTION

Effective leadership has evolved as a key factor in building successful organizations. This book has come about because of our desire to help organizations realize their potential. What does this mean? Every organization seeks to "optimize" its potential and to create its own "competitive advantage." Why is it, then, that so many *potentially* successful organizations fall below expectations? Running an organization is not rocket science, in spite of the literally millions of books designed to help individuals and organizations improve what they are doing. Our society spends billions of dollars on developing software systems and sending people on training programs; future leaders are exposed to intensive levels of education, often spending time away from families on MBA programs designed to help them perform more effectively. Why is it, then, that all of these investments so often fail to deliver the desired outcomes?

1

"So, does anyone else feel that their needs aren't being met?"

Cheney, Tom New Yorker © Tom Cheney/
The New Yorker Collection - www.cartoonbank.com

We believe our approach offers an alternative; in creating this book, we have taken an integrated view of organizational performance that blends a focus on both outcomes (the need to get results) and relationships (the need to create interdependent, cooperative, and collaborative cultures). We have also taken into account something that someone suggested many years ago. We were having a discussion with a client on the difference between training and education, and before we could respond, our two teenage daughters came home from school and said, "Dad, today we had sex education." About two weeks later, they came home and said, "Dad, today we had sex training." What was the difference?

2

Education helps us understand why things happen, whereas training helps us learn new skills and knowledge and apply them.

There has been a lot of scientific research on how adults learn, and the key to this is typically that there must be a connection between the real world in which people live and the new ideas and knowledge that are being taught. Of course, the experience of moving through this learning must be enjoyable, and there might even need to be an emotional connection for the information to be retained and ultimately applied. We present first the "education" piece as we try to establish a context for our ideas based on the changes many of us experience in real life. Hopefully, we will create some "head nodding" as readers connect with the day-to-day challenges that they face and the experiences that have formed their individual history.

Once we have created this context, we will suggest a framework for developing and applying an improved approach to organizational leadership and management; through applying these approaches, we believe that readers will start to develop the "Ah ha" moment, when the simplicity of our ideas begins to crystallize. We will not just provide philosophy and conceptual approaches; we will also add practical tools and direction that our clients have used to put our methods into practice. Finally, we will present a number of case studies of organizations that we have worked with; these case studies show how to apply our ideas and also demonstrate measurable improvements in the day-to-day activities of the organization *plus* measurably improved outcomes from the organizational activity. *A key to our approach is the recognition that while working in a positive environment is more fun, to succeed, the outcome of good working relationships* must *be greater success in task execution.*

Each of us brings a very different background to both this book and to our clients. Peter has established himself as a leading practitioner in the field of humanistic counseling psychology and group work; he puts this extensive practical experience to use in both his clinical practice (The Counseling Institute), where he practices relational psychotherapy, and in his organizational work (from health care to manufacturing organizations) with boards, senior executives, management and leadership teams, and individual employees. Peter's doctoral dissertation on narcissism and attachment has a direct relationship to the issues that we discuss, and his extensive experience in the mental health field, along with his studies and practice in the areas of clinical social work and humanistic psychology, all provide a solid theoretical and technical background for understanding human behavior, and guess what? Organizations are, in fact, collections of people!

"An organization is where a group of different individuals with different talents comes together for the intention of achieving a common purpose."

Given that people form the foundation of any organization, it follows that understanding human behavior and enhancing the ability of people to work together must be a core competitive advantage of a successful organization.

Nick, on the other hand, comes from the "other side of the tracks"; in this partnership, Nick's background in finance and accounting, as well as his in-depth experience in several other areas, provides a very practical, results-oriented focus to the work that we do. Nick spent over twenty years in accounting, with increasing levels of responsibility; he rose to become the vice president of finance and administration of a privately owned industrial distribution business, and as an outcome of this role, he spent three years as the organization's president. He also spent six years as the vice president of finance of the Canadian subsidiary of a major US-based technology multi-national. Add to this his early experience in the retailing business and in the engineering areas of the entertainment and hotel business, plus the past twenty years as a management consultant, and his focus is definitely on the tangible aspects of getting the job done.

Peter and Nick came together over twenty years ago through a mutual friend in the consulting business. First impressions were, naturally, based on perceptions. Nick viewed Peter as dealing with the "soft stuff," while Peter viewed Nick as a "black and white—no area in between" bean counter. Over twenty years later, we have both come to learn that both aspects are critical to business success, and, in fact, the ideas presented in this book, as well as those shared with our clients, have taught us that it is not an "either/or" approach that works but one that combines the human dimensions of performance improvement with an effective focus on organizational outcomes.

As Nick has been prone to say recently, the work that Peter does is incredibly valuable and interesting, but so what? If the outcome is *not* a more effective organization, what does it really achieve? We believe this provides a competitive advantage to our approach, knowing that the authors have very different perspectives!

Let's move now to the business and social environment we find ourselves in. What Nick also accepts now, which Peter always knew, is that in fact, the people stuff *is* the <u>hard stuff</u>. The ideas in this book may be simple conceptually, but application and sustainability will be hard. Some of these ideas are included in the foundational commitments that form the basis of the globally recognized Toyota Management System (TMS), but we have now embedded the overall concepts into our own management model, RP5 (see the appendix). We believe that this framework offers an integrated yet simple approach that almost any organization can embrace and apply.

Further background on both authors is contained in the appendix.

The Changing Business Environment

Plenty of books have been written on the changing face of the economy—be it from a technological, social, global, demographic, or other perspective. What we want to focus on is the shift from a tangible economy to one based on intangibles. This shift is not new and has been developing for almost twenty years—in fact, it heralds the shift from the latter stages of the industrial economy to the early stages of the knowledge society. The "dot com" crash of the 1990s was a precursor, a bump in the road if you like, toward the recognition that the systems and approaches to management and leadership that worked in the past will not work in today's knowledge-based society. Peter's focus has in fact been on the intangibles: the ability of organizations to create value-adding relationships both internally and externally; Nick's concerns and focus have been on the inability of the accounting profession generally, and corporate accountability and performance measurement specifically, to account for the growing importance of intangibles to organizational performance. The impact on organizational value is significant, as shown in the Global Enterprise Value chart; however, never forget that whether an organization is "for profit" or "not for profit," its ability to harness human potential is a growing aspect of effectiveness.

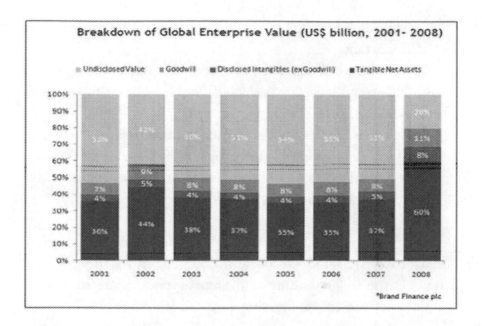

Figure 1.

Chart courtesy Brand Finance, "Intangible Finance Tracker 2009"
(Brand Finance, 2009)

Figure 1 shows how enterprise value during the last decade (excepting the financial meltdown in 2008, which has essentially already been corrected) has increasingly been attributed to intangibles. What does this mean? First, this survey, conducted annually by Brand Finance, looked at the market value (i.e., what investors believed the organization was worth in terms of market valuation) versus the "book value" (i.e., the value as shown in the organization's statement of assets and liabilities, which is presented as a part of the mandatory annual financial statements) of the global top ten thousand public companies—worth in aggregate over $50 trillion. What does this tell us?

1. The value of tangible assets is continuing to become less important.
2. The value of intangibles is becoming more important.
3. This trend is well established (looking back a further ten years will reveal the same pattern).
4. Reliance on financial statements and financial reporting of an organization's value is becoming less important (i.e., accounting data only shows us a limited aspect of how well an organization is actually performing).

Deeper investigation will reveal that while financial measurement is reasonably well understood and codified with standards and protocols, the understanding of intangibles is less understood and certainly not subject to effective quantification and codification. Many of the concepts that underpin this book are not new; the commitment to principles of Total Quality Management (TQM, Mahoney, 1994) started in the 1950s and 1960s; customer satisfaction was written about in the 1970s and 1980s by authors such as Tom Peters (*In Search of Excellence* and *A Passion for Excellence*) and Jan Carlzon of SAS (*Moments of Truth*); the development of organizational models for excellence such as the Baldrige Award; the work on knowledge management and intellectual capital by Karl Sveiby (Sveiby, 1997), Leif Edvinsson (Edvinsson, 1997), Tom Stewart (Stewart, 1997), and Baruch Lev (Lev, 2003); work on value chains by Michael Porter; and work by others on lean thinking. One of the more recent books on this subject by Mary Adams and Michael Oleksak[1] (2010) provides a good background into the emerging issue of intangibles and demonstrates some of the emerging aspects of understanding this critical area. All of these changes are building blocks to a new

---

[1]   Mary Adams and Michael Oleksak. *Intangible Capital*. Santa Barbara, CA: Praeger. 2010.

economy, where a new set of operating paradigms is needed. At the pinnacle of this is the need for a whole new approach to corporate governance (see Nick's 2005 book on the subject, *Governance, Accountability, and Sustainable Development: A New Agenda for the 21st Century*[2]).

This trend is important because a core aspect of an organization's intangible value depends upon its ability to create, maintain, and sustain effective relationships, both internally and externally. We believe that the trend shown in figure 2 illustrates the significance of this.

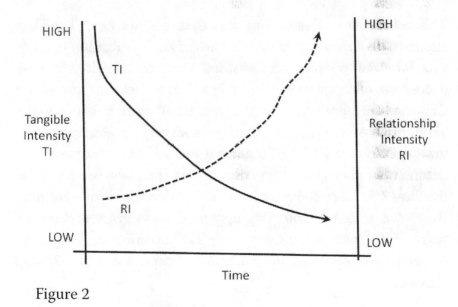

HIGH

TI

Tangible
Intensity
TI

RI

LOW

HIGH

Relationship
Intensity
RI

LOW

Time

Figure 2

As the importance of tangible assets decreases, the importance of effective relationships increases. Why is this? Because relationships enable the effective development of intangible value;

---

[2]   Nick Shepherd. *Governance, Accountability, and Sustainable Development: A New Agenda for the 21st Century*. Toronto: Carswell Thomson. 2005.

9

key intangibles that contribute to an organization's increasing intangible intensity include an engaged, creative, and innovative workforce; loyal and valued customers; suppliers who are treated as partners; interdepartmental activities that are collaborative and cooperative; and effective communications that underpin the sharing of information for the good of the whole organization. Effective leadership creates an organizational culture that is "change ready" and has the agility to move in response to rapidly changing conditions. A key reason why smaller organizations can often outperform larger ones is that they have stronger relationships between their component elements.

The sad aspect to this evolution is that it is not new! The little applied Tribal theory suggests that when an organization exceeds two hundred people, relationships start to deteriorate. One proponent of this approach was Frank Stronach, the successful Canadian entrepreneur who built Magna into a global force in the automotive parts industry. Frank established a solid foundation in the early days of his organization; he built independent, autonomous plants using the Tribal theory and placed emphasis on the local managers being accountable for developing and running their own business unit; this approach was complemented by "partnering" with employees through the creation of a corporate "charter of rights" that established an employee profit-sharing scheme.

The seeds of the decline of General Motors were sown over twenty years ago; relationships with dealers as well as suppliers were heavily adversarial rather than based on a partnering approach. While the short-term outcomes were being celebrated as a result of programs such as supplier cost reduction, led by Ignacio Lopez, the corporation's supply chain was headed for discontent and failure. Many GM suppliers ended up in Chapter 11 even before GM itself was forced to accept its inability to sustain operations.

GM, along with many other manufacturers, went through major changes in the 1970s and 1980s as competition from the Japanese increased; in particular, this era focused on the development of quality management. Global gurus in the quality movement such as J. Edwards Deming (Walton, 1986) focused even at that time on the importance of building effective relationships. Deming's fourteen principles (shown below) demonstrated that effective organizational change must come from a holistic approach, which includes relationship building.

1. Create constancy of purpose for improvement of product and service.
2. Adopt the new philosophy.
3. Cease dependence on mass inspection.
4. End the practice of awarding business on price tag alone.
5. Improve constantly and forever the system of production and service.
6. Institute training.
7. Institute leadership.
8. Drive out fear.
9. Break down barriers between staff areas.
10. Eliminate slogans, exhortations, and targets for the workforce.
11. Eliminate numerical quotas.
12. Remove barriers to pride of workmanship.
13. Institute a vigorous program of education and retraining.
14. Take action to accomplish the transformation.

Many organizations ultimately failed to achieve their potential for quality improvement because they failed to focus on the challenging task of behavioral change, which is at the heart of effective relationships.

Mergers and acquisitions (M&As) is another area where the failure to address relationship management has been shown to be critical. This is especially true in service organizations where substantial sums of money change hands based on valuations that are heavily biased toward intangibles. Because the value paid by the acquiring organization often significantly exceeds the financial or book value of the entity being acquired, the extra amount paid has to go somewhere on the accounting records, so it is entered into an account called "Goodwill." This amount often exceeds billions of dollars, which must be validated by the accountants every year to ensure the amount has not been impaired. While the profession has developed many approaches to try and assess this, it remains an elusive asset to attribute an accurate value to.

The tragedy for shareholders and investors is that over 50 percent of M&As fail to achieve their projected benefits, and, in fact, these amounts are often written off as a loss. Why does this happen? Because organizational culture and human relationships in creating competitive advantage are not well understood, and often the acquiring company, in its efforts to integrate the two entities, actually destroys the inherent competitive advantage of the acquired entity.

Another important dimension of this need for change can be seen in the emerging area of corporate social responsibility (CSR). Organizations such as Ben & Jerry's and the Body Shop voluntarily expanded accountability to the public and believed that organizational success had to be assessed in more than financial terms—in fact, it was around this time that the expression "the triple bottom line"[3] came into being. These organizations accepted that financial performance was important, but that in and of itself this was no assurance of organizational sustainability. They believed that "people, planet, and profit" was a more effective measure of performance. Even before this time, many successful organizations had established statements of organizational "values" that complemented what they did with how they behaved. A classic example is Johnson & Johnson, an organization whose long-term commitment placed primary emphasis on "safety of the public" (see J&J Credo[4]); as a result, in 1982, J&J took a significant financial write-off over the Tylenol scandal rather than tarnish their reputation.

As the public has become more skeptical about corporate ethics and behavior, reputations and brands have been tarnished; customer loyalty has been reduced through problems such as outsourcing to less developed countries, resulting in the unplanned use of child labor. Purchasers become more concerned about being associated with an organization whose behavior appears inconsistent with current social values. As a result, over time the intangible value of the business entity starts to decline. Moving forward, there are already signs that people entering the workforce today are more discriminating in what type of organization they choose to work for based on the employer's commitment to corporate social responsibility. If you start to lose key employees, then the core of innovation and creativity starts to drain away.

---

[3]   The Triple Bottom Line was originally attributed to John Elkington in 1995.

[4]   http://www.jnj.com/connect/about-jnj/jnj-credo.

The Need for a New Paradigm

An organization operating in the twenty-first century is different from one that operated during the Industrial Revolution. Yesterday's focus was on optimizing tangible assets; measuring capacity utilization and equipment downtime; focusing on constantly reducing costs by re-engineering products, services, and processes; and reporting to shareholders on the value of the tangible assets.

Today's focus is on optimizing human potential; people are the enablers of most aspects of intangible value. People develop relationships with suppliers, customers, distributors, and other third parties through which work is executed. People think up new ideas that contribute to new products and services; people also constantly think about the work that they do and seek to find ways to improve effectiveness. People are at the core of an organization's ability to create loyalty and trust. Stephen Covey used to talk about the emotional bank account (EBA) in building strong interpersonal relationships; today, we can extend this to relationships between suppliers and purchasers and between sellers and their customers.

In 2009 and early 2010, Toyota hit a rough patch of poor quality and substantial product recalls. This was a shock to both the company and its competition, but it illustrated the problem that leaders often encounter: arrogance. In a Wharton Business School interview[5] between John Paul MacDuffie of the Wharton Management Department (Interview, 2010) and Professor Takahiro Fujimoto of the University of Tokyo, it was suggested that at the core of

---

[5] "Under the Hood at Toyota's Recall: 'A tremendous Expansion of Complexity.'" Knowledge @Wharton. March 31, 2010.

Toyota's problems was a breakdown in relationships between those dealing with the clients and those in the head office whose job it was to respond to problems. However, the Big Three, in particular GM, took direct aim at Toyota's problems in its advertising in the expectation that customers would leave Toyota and buy "North American"; while some consumers did, it was revealing that in several interviews with Toyota customers, many placed the quality problems in the wider context of having a trusting relationship with Toyota and expressing a willingness to stay loyal because "overall the company can be trusted to solve the problem and continue to provide a good, high quality value for money product." This was the result of years of building client relationships and making investments in the emotional bank account.

In the next chapter, we will present a model that forms the foundation of our approach to organization building through which effective optimization can be achieved. Through this approach, any organization can become more effective. If you are a for-profit organization, this approach will help you develop a framework for competitive advantage; it should enable you to improve internal and external relationships and, through this, improve employee engagement, foster innovation and creativity, and develop stronger and more beneficial relationships with all the third parties that you deal with. It will enhance your outcomes and optimize the capability of your organization to do more with less.

If you are a not-for-profit organization operating in the private sector, these ideas should help you develop a clearer consensus of your organization's mission and vision, and streamline your ability to attract volunteers and make better use of your scarce resources.

If you are a public sector organization, these ideas will help you establish leadership-development approaches that enhance your ability to achieve your organizational mission and provide effective services to your key stakeholders.

If you are reading this as an interested individual, then the key question is, "What can I do to make a difference?" Change is within us, and many people, not in leadership positions per se, can still exert a significant influence on their organization's culture and, through this, its collective ability to function effectively. In effect, you might be able to be the change agent that starts the journey to a new and better place.

CHAPTER 2

"PARTNERS IN SUCCESS": WHY TASK AND RELATIONSHIP?

Organizations don't exist in isolation; they are created to "do stuff," to generate results, and as such, they tend to be task focused. An army exists to fight battles, and its goal is to win the war; a producer of goods and services exists to create and sell products and services, and it is successful by attracting and keeping customers and making a profit at doing it. Not-for-profit organizations are created to fill specific needs, and they are successful when they satisfy those needs to the greatest extent possible within the funding available.

An organization of any type is typically composed of a group of people who come together to make something happen. For decades, management thinking has focused heavily on the effective execution of tasks to produce results. Many of the tools offered by management gurus have focused on increasing task effectiveness. Examples include software systems and approaches such as quality management, process management, and business process re-engineering. In addition, reporting in many cases is heavily task focused, utilizing areas such as output per person, units shipped, and cycle time. Even at the national level, a country's effectiveness is demonstrated by its gross national product, based on its output of goods and services. Management style has also traditionally been focused on getting results and the management of people developed as a "command and control" school. Organizations raise money to hire people and purchase equipment, and then they bring people and equipment (machines, tools, and other tangible facilities) together to make it work and deliver the desired results.

Historically, many organizations relied upon focusing their management attention on task; effectiveness was seen to be a result of management's ability to control and direct operations, to plan and organize. The people in the business followed instructions to a great degree; the manager was seen as the knowledge worker, and other employees were the labor force. People in these positions were traditionally less qualified than management and supported the equipment and systems to generate results. Management's focus on task often resulted in creating demands on the workforce, which had limited leverage, as they could be easily replaced, and this created the need for worker representation through the creation of unions. In many organizations, this gradually devolved into adversarial relationships between owners and managers, who needed to improve task effectiveness, and the workforce, who believed that the demands being made to achieve these results were socially unreasonable or that the formula for sharing financial rewards was unfair.

The economic environment continued to change; manufacturing remained important, and to increase competitiveness, many organizations automated their tasks, in order to reduce their labor costs and increase productivity, quality, and consistency. After all, went some schools of thought, you just need to set up a machine and turn it on, and it works almost continuously, without argument and coffee breaks! The future of competitiveness was seen to be in automation. But what was happening was that while direct labor (those workers in the unskilled or semiskilled position) declined, the need for higher skilled technicians, electronics experts, programmers, and others started to rise as equipment became more complex. What was building was a base of intangible assets that complemented and supported the tangible equipment; in fact, without these people, the equipment was not really worth much. There is a great example given in Thomas Stewart's *Intellectual Capital: The New Wealth of Organizations,*[6] which discussed how Alan Benjamin, former director of the SEMA Group (a leading computer services company), recast SEMA's financial results to treat traditional tangible assets as consumables, and the costs of the workforce were being split between current costs (to earn current revenues) and costs associated with the future (e.g., building relationships and other intangibles).

At the same time, another sector of the economy was growing quickly; this is often referred to as the service sector. This includes organizations such as banks, insurance companies, and financial services firms; in addition, manufacturers were also growing their "service" segments, such as dealerships that sold and supported vehicles, and post-sales support for electronic equipment. Governments also continued to grow as well as social agencies and not-for-profit organizations. While these organizations didn't really manufacture anything per se, they did require tangible assets to support their service tasks, items such as computer systems for service delivery; computer-aided design and manufacturing systems for product design and development; and delivery

---

[6]   Thomas Stewart. *Intellectual Capital: The New Wealth of Organizations.* New York: Currency/Doubleday. 1997.

vans and trucks (as an example, FedEx is a service business yet needs tangible assets to execute that delivery service). These organizations also had a "task execution" requirement, which had to be executed effectively in order to deliver the required results or outcomes.

In the 1970s, the global energy crisis plus the emergence of Japan as a leader in the production of high-quality products generated a focus on both quality management initiatives and customer service programs. CEOs supported the allocation of significant resources into areas such as Total Quality Management (TQM) initiatives that focused on implementing new equipment for checking and validating production quality; Statistical Process Control (SPC) was implemented to track and monitor the effectiveness of processes through which products were manufactured. New processes were implemented to ensure that suppliers were chosen for their ability to comply with specifications as well as meet competitive prices. Training budgets were reinforced to include all employees in the new quality programs. Yet for many companies, these initiatives failed to deliver the expected results.

There was also an extensive focus on improving task management in the service business through customer-service initiatives. Ideas such as process-improvement teams and quality circles were adopted from manufacturers. Service process mapping was implemented. Training programs were developed to teach employees how to deliver high-quality customer service. Yet again, many programs failed to deliver the anticipated results.

During this period, two underlying business concepts were being developed in Japan. These initiatives were, in fact, the secret of how both quality initiatives and service improvement could actually be implemented and deliver actual, sustainable results.

The first was Hoshin Kanri (Akao, 1991), which is an approach to business planning; the second was the Toyota Management System (TMS; Liker, 2004). Both of these initiatives took a holistic approach to organizational management that recognized that task alone cannot deliver high level effectiveness. We will discuss both concepts in a little more detail later.

Surveys in North America reveal that typical organizations are about 80 percent focused on task execution; the problem is that these surveys also show that the same organizations are only about 30 percent focused on building relationships that support effective task execution. (These numbers, in our experience, vary to some degree based on national culture, but in most cases, the relationship between the two remains valid.) The association between task and relationship was discussed in various works by Lefton, Buzzotta, and Sherberg[7] about their Dimensional Model of Human Behavior (2005), a diagram of which is shown in figure 3. In addition, the work of Ken Blanchard (2007) and others in leadership focuses on the task-relationship (T-R) concept.

---

[7]   V. Ralph Buzzotta, Robert Eugene Lefton and Manuel Sherberg. *Effective Selling Through Psychology: The Dimensional Sales Model.* New York: Wiley. 1972. Robert Eugene Lefton and Victor Buzzotta. *Leadership Through People Skills: Dimensional Management Strategies.* Toronto: Psychological Associates. 2003.

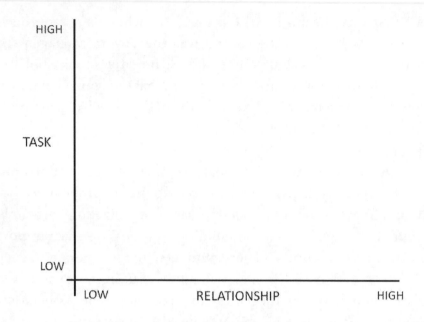

This framework identifies that human behavior is a combination of task focus and relationship focus and that individual behavior can be placed at any position between high and low dimensions on either attribute (as Blanchard indicates, it is "situational"). Organizations tend to be created to focus on tasks—getting the job done with a degree of focused zeal. Individuals have a choice but typically are social beings that appear to be more driven by relationships. (While Peter's counseling practice traditionally focused on building or repairing relationships, Nick's work traditionally focused on looking at how to execute task more effectively to lower costs per unit, increase sales, or generate more profits; as professionals, our fields of work were very different!)

The value of an organization depends upon outcomes or results; a well-run for-profit business produces results that investors appreciate and so attribute a value of "future earnings" to the organization. A well-run not-for-profit produces outcomes consistent with its mission at a competitive cost. To enable this success, organizations increasingly depend upon intangible assets, in particular their people, who build relationships both internally and externally.

Today's challenge is that those responsible for organizational oversight, such as boards of directors and investors, continue to place heavy emphasis on an organization's financial results to assess its capacity to continue to operate effectively. Securities legislation and accounting professionals have, to some degree, addressed this issue through having management provide a written commentary (called a management discussion and analysis, or MD&A), combined with a requirement during an audit to assess an organization's ability to operate as a "going concern." The challenge is that financial results focus on lagging indicators—what has happened. North American corporations have suffered for years with something called "short-termism," or focusing on quarterly earnings; to a degree, this has encouraged internal decisions to optimize short-term earnings while depleting the capacity to sustain future competitiveness. Across the board, cutting of costs is often the cause of depleting intangible capital. As a result of organizational oversight focusing on financial results, management also tends to focus on "managing by the numbers," resulting in less attention to internal and external relationships.

The reality is that people, who work better within relational environments, are the ones who execute the tasks necessary to deliver outcomes and, through this, obtain financial results. The problem has been that no matter what new approaches, tools, and ideas are brought to bear on the execution of task, they often fall short of their potential because of their inability to engage the people. The importance of this concept has never been greater; competition is global, with emerging economies with lower labor costs challenging traditional industrial economies. These states are now shifting their focus to the knowledge economy, which is seen as the emerging frontier of economic growth and competitiveness. Some nations have a greater challenge than others, and this is because of national culture. America is symbolized by the "Marlboro Man" striking out on his own as an independent survivor, dependent on no one; this is "how the West was won"; this is how competition thrives through the survival of the fittest; it is about winners and losers. Other nationalities, in particular some of those in Asia and South America, developed as more collaborative states; in these cultures, relationships come before task.

Greg Mortenson[8] may not be known to many business professionals, yet his first book, *Three Cups of Tea*, coauthored with David Relin (2007), was on the *New York Times* bestseller list for three years. This work focuses on his efforts and successes in building schools for children in Pakistan and Afghanistan; what is so important is how he demonstrates that any success in such a venture must come *first* from building relationships. "Three cups of tea" refers to the cultural approach in which "when we share the first cup of tea, you are a stranger; the second cup of tea shared is with a friend, and the third cup you have become family." Greg makes the point that military strategies in countries such as Afghanistan and Iraq cannot be successfully resolved by force alone; building relationships and getting to know the people who live, love, and stay in these countries must form a core strategy for long-term change.

Earlier, we identified two approaches that have existed for years and that have brought success through combining task and

---

[8] There has been some recent controversy about the accuracy of Mortenson's accounts of what occurred but the authors tend to endorse the overall account and the principles involved.

relationship. First, Hoshin Kanri; the book of the same name was originally published in Japan in 1988, and the English translation[9] was published in 1991. In the publisher's message at the front of the book, a loose translation of the term "Hoshin Kanri" is presented: "Hoshin means shining metal, compass or pointing the direction; Kanri means management or control. Hoshin is often translated as policy, but it refers to something more far-reaching, like the vision, purpose, or long-term direction of the company." Compaq Computer was an early North American adopter of this strategy (Compaq was later purchased by HP, who also used this management approach); other firms included Proctor and Gamble, Intel, and Xerox. The Baldrige Award also reflects aspects of the Hoshin Kanri approach in its planning dimensions.

Hoshin Kanri came about in Japan in the early 1950s because management was beginning to understand the process issues related to quality problems. Changes were required in the organizational culture; in other words, while the task aspects were clear, they were having trouble translating the intent into what people were actually paying attention to. What was needed was an approach that engaged people in the execution of task. This approach included a core focus on clear accountability and responsibility throughout the organization, including the empowerment of those working on task to plan and manage their own work. This started to change the dimension of management control to one of communication and engagement.

The second, and probably more enduring framework, has been the development of the Toyota Management Principles,[10] which demonstrate the foundation upon which Toyota built its global

---

[9]   Yoji Akao. *Hoshin Kanri: Policy Deployment for Successful TQM.* Cambridge, MA: Productivity Press. 1991.

[10]   Jeffrey Liker. *The Toyota Way.* New York: McGraw-Hill. 2004.

organization. Jeffrey Liker's book shows a pyramid structure that reflects his "4P" model that forms the basis of Toyota's approach to management. The first "P" is "Philosophy," which focuses on long-term strategic thinking. This is foundational, in that it provides a constancy of purpose. (Jim Collins also refers to successful organizations as having this basic type of foundation.)

The second "P" is for "Process": the area through which task is executed. TMP applies a focused approach to designing and managing task execution through process management, including traditional tools, such as SPC, but also current approaches, such as lean management techniques. This area focuses on zero waste, with a focus on flow, as well as clearly defined responsibilities and accountabilities, including the ability of any employee (associate) to stop the line when process problems occur. The core thinking focuses on task management as being the activity that utilizes effective processes to get the job done. While many other organizations have adopted these task-focused approaches, including Six Sigma, business process re-engineering, lean management, and others, it is in fact the next "P" in the pyramid that makes the difference and, in our view, creates the competitive advantage.

The third "P" is focused on "People and Partners," which in Toyota terms is "Respect and Teamwork." A key word here is "respect," as it applies to not only internal people, but also all other partners, including suppliers. In the late 1990s and early 2000s, we spent considerable time working with automotive suppliers and saw a significant difference in how organizations like Toyota and Honda partnered with their suppliers versus the strategies of the Big Three, GM in particular. Many will remember Lopez's supplier cost-reduction initiatives. In his recent book,[11] David Anderson (2010) discusses how the approaches of organizations such as GM failed to achieve lasting cost reductions and, in fact, had the opposite effect: some suppliers hid their innovative approaches from GM. As the old song says, "It ain't what you do, it's the way that you do it!" No buyer can afford *not* to go after lower and lower costs. However, lasting change comes from building relationships with suppliers that are based on mutual respect and collaboration. GM's adversarial management approach sowed the seeds of its own demise well over twenty years ago.

Within the third "P" that we discuss here is the importance of leadership, those who convert intent to execution (e.g., those responsible for task must share the principles relative to both task outcomes as well as approaches). In the late 1990s, General Electric modified its approach of evaluating the performance of managers, because it realized that some managers were getting the desired results *plus* building effective long-term relationships with partners (in particular, employees), while others achieved results but were systematically destroying the organization's ability to build intangible assets (i.e., people and relationships) for the future. The following table indicates how these two approaches to high task achievement were portrayed; the cell on the upper left (Type IV) deals with what we will discuss later as "high task, low relationship," whereas the cell on the upper right (Type I) is "high task, high relationship." Both achieve results (i.e., task outcomes that meet requirements), but the one on the right perpetuates an organizational culture.

---

[11]　Dr. David M. Anderson. *Design for Manufacturability & Concurrent Engineering.* Cambria, CA: CIM Press. 2010.

Task orientation	**Type IV.** Those that make the numbers but don't share our values. Making the call on these managers is the most difficult of all – they deliver results but "...they do it while ignoring values. They are a destructive force because they poison the environment, wear people down, stifle creativity, and cause valuable talent down the line to flee GE"	**Type I.** Not only delivers on performance commitments but believes in and furthers GE's small company values. These are the "A" players who will represent the core of the future leadership into the next century.
	Type II. Does not meet commitments and do not share our values – nor last long at GE.	**Type III.** Believes in the values but sometimes misses the commitments. These managers are usually coached, encouraged, and given another chance.
	Relationship orientation	

Note: The chart is based on an approach adopted by GE in the late 1990s that addressed the challenge of recognizing and rewarding high task/high relationship managers versus high task/low relationship managers.

Jeffrey Liker wrote another book on Toyota about the importance of sustaining an organizational culture as an underpinning of successful task execution.[12] In this book with Michael Hoseus, Liker discusses the challenge of taking an organizational culture, initially developed in Japan, and applying it globally. The first chapter, "The DNA of Toyota Lies in Its Culture," sets the stage for the remainder of the book.

Finally, the fourth "P" deals with a culture of continual improvement. While many organizations have tried to implement suggestion

---

[12]   Jeffrey Liker and Michael Hoseus. *Toyota Culture: The Heart and Soul of the Toyota Way.* New York: McGraw-Hill. 2008.

schemes and approaches to engage employees in improvement initiatives, few achieve the success of Toyota. Why? Because without the underlying "Ps" that we have discussed, there is no real reason for people to commit to being involved. This brings us right back to the early work of Liker that deals with selling skills; change management is about selling and implementing ideas. Although now part of e-mail language, the term "WIIFM" initially meant "What's In It For Me?", relative to selling something to a buyer. Failure to answer this question results in SW^{2}C: "So What? Who Cares?" Unless partners in the business are somehow engaged in the business, then change will not take root.

So here we have a proven approach to bringing together a number of factors to build organizational effectiveness and, through this, achieve success. We believe that the foundation of this approach is, in fact, the ability to work on both the task dimension (getting stuff done) and the relationship dimension (how we behave) in unison. Further than this, we believe that we can only achieve success in relationships if we strive to understand human behavior and, through this, build a foundation of communication, collaboration, coordination, and commitment. These are the skills that we will expand on in the remainder of this book.

CHAPTER 3

THE CHANGING FACE OF "TASK"

Over the past decade or more, every type of organization has been faced with increased competition; for business, excess capacity and globalization have leveled the playing field, and the market for high labor content products and services had been tilted in terms of shifting production to lower cost economies. All other aspects of economies have seen the trickle-down results; not-for-profits have seen their fundraising reduced and are faced with doing more with less; there is pressure on governments for minimal tax increases at all levels; in fact, even tax reductions have strained the public sector.

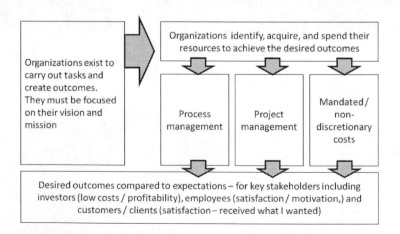

Add to these changes at the macroeconomic level in particular the impact of demographic changes, and an aging population, and we see additional demands that call for diverting funding to these areas. We can begin to see that the resources available to be applied to doing work are being strained everywhere. Organizations "do stuff"—that's what they are there for! In a for-profit organization, the goal is to come up with products and services that people will see a value in and, as a result, purchase them. If the organization is well run and the pricing correctly set, revenues will exceed costs and provide owners with a profit on their investment. Organizations typically have limited resources that they can apply to doing the stuff that they do; work is typically done through applying resources to processes, projects, or other costs as shown above. While there is no general rule, many, if not most, organizations conduct their work through repetitive activities, which are referred to as "processes." Some estimates set the allocation of resources to process management at up to 70 percent; projects are also a consumer of resources, and again, the amount assigned to projects varies. Processes include manufacturing processes, service delivery, and loan applications; they can also refer to internal processes such as hiring processes, payment processes, and many, many others. The main difference between processes and projects is that processes are turned on every time a transaction takes place, whereas projects usually are assigned funding on a one-time basis; when the project is finished, the funding goes away. We often have to assign some resources to what are called "non-value-adding" uses such as paying audit fees and taxes (we refer to them as non-value adding because they are not a direct part of executing the work required to create and deliver products and services).

Faced with a squeeze in resource availability, organizations have been seeking out ways to more effectively undertake the work that they do. The great success of organizations such as the Project Management

Institute has come during a period when people are trying to more effectively manage projects; this is an interesting phenomenon, as the greater the level of change in an organization, the more change-management projects that are undertaken! Thus there is a greater need for effective project-management techniques.

When we look at processes, we see an area where task becomes really critical; major organizational resources go into task work that is executed through processes. Attention to effectiveness in these areas has seen the rise of interest in quality management, process management, cycle time management, lean management, and many, many more initiatives.

The purpose of every one of these initiatives is to allow organizations to use their limited resources more effectively. It is interesting to note that the American Society for Quality (ASQ) has always promoted the application of quality management not only as a means of obtaining "compliance with requirements" (e.g., meeting specifications with zero defects and achieving customer satisfaction as benefits), but also as a direct linkage between the absence of quality as a cause of excess costs (i.e., poor quality wastes resources).

Historically, quality gurus such as Dr. Deming and Dr. Juran (Frank, 1951) have lectured organizations on the need for quality as a competitive advantage. The following list shows the last fifty years of the quality movement's efforts to enhance organizational effectiveness through focusing on the benefits of reducing the costs of poor quality.

- 1951: Dr. Juran publishes *Quality Control Handbook* (1951), citing "Gold in the Mine."
- 1961: Dr. Feigenbaum publishes *Total Quality Control.*

- 1961: ASQ creates "Quality Costs Committee" (to convince business that quality saves money rather than adding cost).
- 1963: US Department of Defense issues its MIL Standard Q9858, indicating it "will not pay for suppliers' mistakes" and making cost of quality a standard requirement.
- 1979: Phil Crosby's *Quality Is Free* demonstrates the significant savings to be achieved through quality improvements.
- 1980s: Cost of quality is used more extensively to measure benefits of continuous improvement initiatives.
- 1994: The Big Three (Ford, GM, Chrysler) issues QS 9000, an automotive quality standard that makes continual improvement a core aspect of quality compliance.
- 1998: ISO 10014 introduces *Guidelines for Realizing Financial and Economic Benefits* for use of management's implementation of quality systems standards.

Today, the American Society for Quality continues with its ongoing focus to link enhanced competitiveness and improved financial performance to quality improvements.

Of particular interest is the fact that as long ago as 1963, the US government realized that waste caused by poor quality would end up in a contractor's cost of doing business and issued procurement guidelines requiring defense contractors to *exclude* the costs caused by poor quality from their recoverable charges to the government. (Sad that today we all continue to pay the costs of a supplier's poor quality caused by poor work planning and execution!)

More recently, solutions such as Six Sigma (Harry, 2000) and lean management (Collection, 2005) have been the religion of the day to help organizations focus on and eliminate waste—wherever it occurs. The reality is that some of these initiatives fail; they become the flavor of the day, and employees seem to develop a resistance to change by saying, "Keep your head down and this too will pass." Yet survival in the face of continuing competitive pressure for resources constantly pushes every organization to enhance their capability to execute their work effectively.

There have been many excellent books written on how to more effectively manage the processes of getting work done in an organization. Examples are *The Execution Premium* by Kaplan and Norton (2008), following on the heels of the excellent work in areas such as Activity-Based Management (Brimson, 1994), Activity-Based Costing (ABC; Cooper, 1993), and Balanced Scorecards (Kaplan, 1996) that have been adopted by many organizations. Another example is *Built to Last* (Collins, 1994), in which Jim Collins focuses on specific strategies to make an organization successful, such as "Good to Great." Development of effective leadership skills is yet another area of focus, with many new books constantly emerging.

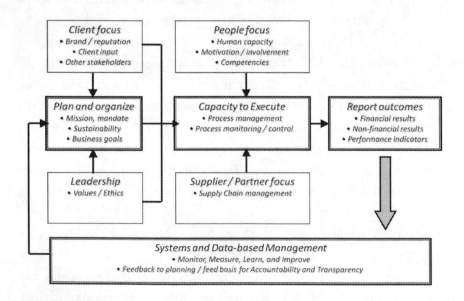

Many of these books attack a specific piece of an organization's approach to business management, yet for many years, a more holistic model has been in place that provides some level of insight to the importance of bringing these aspects of business together. While there are critics of these management models, they have stood the test of time; what is more, there is an emerging consensus from these models about what organizations need to focus on to be well run. In the United States, the best known model is the Baldrige criteria for performance excellence, which establishes the core criteria that any organization can use to improve overall performance. The chart shows the key criteria that are typically focused on in assessing organizational performance.

These criteria apply not only to manufacturing and service businesses, both large and small, but also to education, health-care, and not-for-profit organizations. Thus the criteria underpin the earlier comment that the search for greater effectiveness is not limited to any segment of the economy. What is interesting is that work we have done indicates that the chosen criteria are in fact about 95 percent common not only across all organizations, but also across *all* awards of excellence on a global basis.

This chart reflects the typical commonality between the US Baldrige with the Award for Excellence criteria adopted by Canada, Europe, and Australia. While groupings and categories, change the content remains similar.

Core Factors	Baldrige (USA)	NQI (Canada)	EFEM (Europe)	ABEF (Australia)
Leadership	Leadership	Leadership	Leadership	Leadership & innovation
Customer / Citizen	Customer focus	Citizen / Client focus	Yes	Customer & market focus
Employees	Workforce focus	People focus	People	People
Planning	Strategic planning	Planning	Strategy	Strategy & planning process
Process	Process management	Process management	Processes, products and services	Processes, products & services
Partners / Suppliers	Yes	Supplier / partner focus	Partnerships & resources	Yes
Results	Results	Organizational performance	People results, customer results, society results, key results	Business results
	Measurement, analysis and knowledge management			Data information & knowledge

Dr. Deming, one of the quality gurus introduced in chapter 1 (including his "fourteen points"), had the foresight to realize that attention to process improvement would only work if it was partnered with attention to the human aspects of an organization's activity.

We can review his fourteen points and start to align them with a more effective focus on an organization's approach to doing business; through this, we can begin to see why holistic approaches to change are the only ones that will work. The chart shows the relationship between Deming's fourteen points and the criteria generally included in assessing organizations for performance excellence; the fit appears quite good: to achieve excellence, one has to take a holistic approach.

Deming's Principle	Leadership	Strategy & Planning	Customer / client	People	Suppliers	Process	Results & Measures
1. Create constancy of purpose for improvement of product or service	PRIMARY						
2. Adopt the new philosophy	PRIMARY						
3. Cease dependence on mass inspection						PRIMARY	
4. End the practice of awarding business on price tag alone					PRIMARY		
5. Improve constantly and forever the system for production and service			PRIMARY				
6. Institute training				PRIMARY			
7. Institute leadership	PRIMARY						
8. Drive out fear	PRIMARY						
9. Break down barriers between staff areas				PRIMARY			
10. Eliminate slogans, exhortations and targets for the workforce	PRIMARY						
11. Eliminate numerical quotas							PRIMARY
12. Remove barriers to pride of workmanship				PRIMARY			
13. Institute a vigorous program of education and re-training		PRIMARY					
14. Take action to accomplish the transformation	PRIMARY						

This over-riding focus on improving task execution has brought many new initiatives to organizations; however, as we will explore next, many of these are becoming more difficult to execute. Why? Because organizations are coming face to face with the realization that a task focus without a corresponding building of relationships will fail to yield the desired benefits.

Consider some of the approaches to improving task effectiveness being employed by organizations today:

- Reducing the numbers of suppliers and consolidating purchasing
- Developing partnerships with suppliers to lower overall costs including sharing of design, development, and administrative information
- Partnering with third parties to deliver products and services including public–private partnerships in government

- Establishing joint ventures with other organizations to pool expertise and business interests
- Outsourcing of whole areas of an organization's business
- Moving toward team-based, interdepartmental process approaches to task execution
- Implementing continual improvement in process enhancement

In addition to the challenges to changing task execution, organizations are also facing changed contexts within which these tasks must be executed; examples include the following:

- Speed of change to which organizations must respond, creating a potential for widening of the gap between leadership understanding of task execution and those on the front lines actually doing the work.
- Growing importance of nontangible assets in driving competitive advantage; examples include customer goodwill and relationships, and employee engagement in driving innovation and improvement.
- Growing importance in community engagement in business expansion and development, including the whole emergence of corporate social responsibility (CSR).

It is clear from the quality movement, as well as from the last thirty years of focusing attention on attributes of management excellence, that these building blocks are well understood. The challenge is, and remains, the ability to apply this knowledge in a way that increases competitiveness. So often, the drive to reduce cost harms relationships.

Follow the Money to Reduce Costs

Where does the money go? If we know this, we can reduce the cost of doing business and therefore meet increased competition and do more with less. The following table shows some examples using (H) High, (M) Medium, and (L) Low intensity:

Examples of organizations	Investment / Capital Cost	Purchased Materials	Direct Labor	Indirect Labor	Other Costs
Manufacturers	H	H	M	M	L
Services	L	L	H	H	M
Retailing	M	H	M	H	M
Not for Profit	L	L	L	H	M
Government	H	M	M	H	L
Education	M	M	H	M	M
Health Care	H	H	H	M	M

So what strategies are under way to mitigate organizational costs? If investment costs are high, the solution might well be to get out of the business or at least outsource the more expensive aspects to third parties; in some cases, this would involve setting up joint ventures with others. In government, for example, direct face-to-face service delivery is being replaced by either services delivered by the private sector or by on-line services provided through the Internet or self-service kiosks.

If material costs are high, then sourcing materials from low-cost suppliers, wherever they may be globally, would be a strategy, possibly changing suppliers to get the lowest prices; another choice would be redesigning products to eliminate certain materials costs, including substitution of lower cost materials.

If labor cost are high, then process streamlining and simplification would be important, and outsourcing some aspects may be an opportunity; as an example, many services organizations as well as manufacturers have outsourced customer service and call centers to less developed countries, where wage rates are much lower. In some cases, the levels of service are reduced to save money.

As these changes take place, they bring with them new challenges in how these tasks are to be managed, and one of the greatest challenges is to develop and sustain positive working relationships with other stakeholders, who have traditionally been managed at arm's length. Let's review some examples.

Value chain management and improvement is a core strategy that many organizations are following to bring down acquisition costs and develop closer working relationships between suppliers, buyers, and end users (customers). The competitiveness of a product or service to the end user is the result of the cost structures and profit levels of the combined members of the supply chain. Thus if a third party can provide post-sales support for a manufacturer's product, the manufacturer may be more competitive if they turn that function over to that organization. Likewise, if the same manufacturer can engage the design skills of their supplier's organization in coming up with more cost-effective designs for component parts, they may turn over a portion of that work to their supplier. In addition, it may speed up the time-to-market for new products and services.

Nowhere is this collaboration more needed than in the area of business administration; many organizations today are striving to reduce administrative costs in areas such as purchasing, accounting, and human-resource management. Computer technology allows many of these tasks to be automated, yet with the massive technology available, why is it so slow to be applied? Because administration is an interdependent function that requires the interchange of data between members of a supply chain. Many organizations still do business on the basis of sending pieces of paper between each other; this requires manual intervention. If buyers and suppliers are able to collaborate and, through this, automate their administrative functions and eliminate manual intervention, major improvements in cost would result. Organizations that have achieved this have significantly lower administrative costs than those that have not achieved it.

As organizations try and do more with fewer resources, they typically focus on where the money goes; we have already established that a significant portion of organizational resources flows into process management, and included in this is payroll, which flows from people doing the work. Thus, reducing payroll costs is often a core focus on improving organizational profitability and effectiveness. In addition, manufacturers (part of the traditional/old industrial economy) have enjoyed costing (financial systems for analysis) that shows exactly where and why labor is being utilized. However, a fast-growing sector of the economy is service business, and the fastest growing cost area is overhead or indirect costs. These areas consume major amounts of payroll costs, yet managers struggle with why the money is being spent. New accounting approaches, such as Activity-Based Costing and Resource Consumption Analysis (RCA), have provided tools to start analyzing these costs, but the ability to understand and start reducing these costs depends almost entirely on a combination of changed human engagement and new systems for data capture. From a tools/task perspective, process management has become the buzzword, but success has eluded those who fail to change their approaches to engaging and leading the workforce.

What are organizations doing to achieve this in the twenty-first century? In the next chapters, we will look at the foundations needed to provide leadership in this organizational shift. Task remains critical, as organizations *must* be effective in what they do, but achieving this rests heavily on a shifted paradigm to human-relationship management, which depends on effective leadership for its success.

CHAPTER 4

SHARED VALUES: FOUNDATION FOR

RELATIONSHIPS

Our research and implementation experience has brought us to the conclusion that building effective relationships that enhance task effectiveness cannot be achieved without two key components. First, as individuals we need to have self-awareness in order to understand ourselves and how (and why) we respond to situations in the way that we do. Second, we need to arrive at some level of mutual agreement on organizational values. Many books have been written on this subject that explores the foundations of principles and values, and while we value much of this work, we will not go through it again here. However, we seek the integration of an effective approach to values-based management in the work that we do.

Some of our thinking in this area comes from a very practical situation that arose when working with a client; this particular company is a family-owned business that has transitioned through to the third generation. This organization operates globally from a small headquarters in Ontario, Canada, and has built a large part of its business through developing 50/50 joint ventures with partners who also form its major customers. In the course of our work with the owners, we were discussing how to put together an effective presentation to prospective international partners, in particular in the emerging markets of eastern and central Europe and Asia. We asked them, "Why would anyone want to partner with you as a preference to anyone else?" While this question could produce defensive responses, it served to stimulate thinking around "What do we stand for as an organization?" The answer to this question can only be found if an organization has a solid grasp of its values and the behavioral principles around which it manages its business.

A similar question arose many years ago at a seminar in Toronto that Nick was giving at the American Management Association (AMA[13]) on the subject of building business partnerships. Much of Nick's work at this time was about the development of value-added partnerships for organizations that were moving beyond traditional buyer/supplier relationships, where the focus was toward mutually beneficial relationships, where each party seeks more than just a supply source. This work has since become mainstream for many organizations, but at that time, it was in the early stage of development. Nick had asked the participants, "Is there anyone actually doing this type of work with your suppliers or customers at the present time?" and two participants from the same (well-known international) company raised their hands and became engaged in deep conversation. Upon being asked what their concern was, it turned out that while they had spent significant resources already on trying to build relationships with suppliers, several of their efforts had ended up in failure. In the course of the discussion, it soon became apparent that while they had mutual business interests, their cultures, values, and belief

---

[13]   AMA operates in the Canadian Management Centre.

systems were significantly different and ended up becoming the source of failure.

What is amazing is that we already know this about human relationships; Peter's work in the counseling side of his professional practice continually reveals that a failure to accept another person and having a minimal level of shared values are often the reasons behind the failure of a relationship or marriage. The question to groups of participants at our training programs, "How many of you married your wife after the first date?" elicits much laughter, yet how often do we attempt to develop business relationships without allowing any time to "get to know each other"?

This aspect of building shared values is becoming increasingly critical as we become more integrated as societies; in the past, individuals lived and worked in fairly well-defined communities and, as such, developed a sense of the values of that community. In many cases, societal/cultural values were developed around a foundation of religious values; in fact, this remains the case in many societies today, which creates challenges when individuals move from one society to a different society. The movie *Bend It Like Beckham* provided a great study in the cultural conflicts within families that can exist when parents emigrate from one culture, where they learned their values, to another country, where the values are different and their children are challenged to manage the conflict between parental expectations and pressure to maintain traditional values and their new peer group. The more immigrant parents sustain their traditional values by interacting with friends from the old country, the greater the challenge for the children.

A great deal of research work is being performed to understand the depth and breadth of societal values, and the chart from the

World Values Survey[14] illustrates the fundamental challenge of integrating people from different cultures and backgrounds.

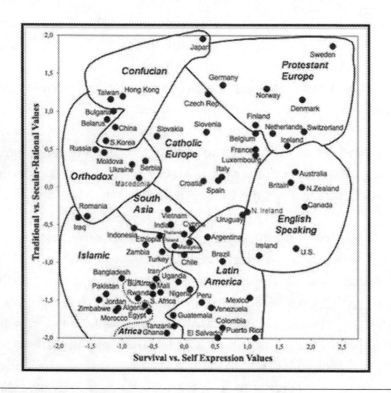

©Inglehart-Welzel Cultural Map of the World, by Ronald Inglehart. This map reflects the fact that a large number of basic values are closely correlated; they can be depicted in just two major dimensions of cross-cultural variation. Source: Ronald Inglehart and Christian Welzel, *Modernization, Cultural Change and Democracy*. New York: Cambridge University Press, 2005, p. 64, based on the World Values Surveys; see www.worldvaluessurvey.org

In the same way that societies need to have a clear understanding of their values, so do organizations; it is unfair and unreasonable for those managing an organization in the twenty-first century to assume that everyone knows what is expected of them in terms of behavior. So how do we put this in place? We have developed

---

[14]   www.worldvaluessurvey.org. for the chart and background.

and applied a process that we believe creates a foundation for success.

Building an Organizational Values Framework

At the outset, it needs to be clear that this is not a "quick fix": building values takes time, and there are few, if any, shortcuts; in fact, failure to allow the necessary time often creates mistrust and lacks integrity. We love this quote from Jim Collins:

> **Executives** spend too much time drafting, wordsmithing, and redrafting vision statements, mission statements, values statements, purpose statements, aspiration statements, and so on. They spend nowhere near enough time trying to align their organizations with the values and visions already in place.

In addition, Colin Powell, former head of the US Joint Chiefs of Staff and also a former US secretary of state, in his treatise on leadership had the following reflection of the importance of getting "the right people on the bus":

> "Organization doesn't really accomplish anything. Plans don't accomplish anything, either. Theories of management don't much matter. Endeavors succeed or fail because of the people involved. Only by attracting the best people will you accomplish great deeds."

Most organizations probably have a set of values, but they are often not widely discussed, understood, or shared. When organizations start out, the owner usually sets the stage for the values, so everyone knows how to act in their day-to-day activities; however, the larger an organization grows and the more people, especially from differing backgrounds, that are added, the more blurred the shared sense of values becomes. Changes in leadership create changes in perceptions around what an organization stands for, where it is going, and what is expected. In *Discovering the Soul of Service* (Berry, 1999), a great book on service management, the author indicated that one of the key factors in building a successful and sustainable service organization was the tenure of the CEO and his or her knowledge of the business. It is interesting that this appears to fly in the face of what is actually practiced today, but it does make sense. If a key aspect of following a leader is learning to know what he or she expects and to develop trust that he or she does what he or she says he or she does, then this takes time, and the constant churn rate of senior executives is, in fact, contributing to the problem of sustainable competitive advantage.

So this is where we start the process of developing organizational values; we don't reinvent the wheel, we simply try to clarify and validate what is already in place. However, this is often a surprise in itself, as the values that the leadership perceives to be those of the organization are often *not* those that the people in the organization actually think exist. We were both involved with a billion-dollar-plus systems company some years ago (it has since been acquired and disappeared!), and we carried out a simple survey. We asked the respondents to choose between seven values, and the results were segregated between senior executives, line managers, and all other employees.

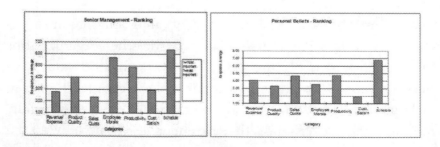

The results were fascinating, in that the perception of senior management about business priorities was quite clearly different from that of the rank and file in the organization. In particular, senior management ranked "employee morale" at about 5.5 on the 10-point scale, whereas the employees' perception was that it ranked about 3.5—quite a difference.

The process we use is best depicted by the following chart that shows four stages: the first stage involves developing, based on input from the organization, an outline of what the core values are believed to be; these results are then validated against organizational leadership's expectations to see whether they agree. Disagreement at this stage results in a longer process of developing a list of values and obtaining agreement of what they should be. This will, of course, create issues, because if there is misalignment between what the values should be and what they appear to be based on internal behaviors, then changes in team members may be required! Key to this activity is a process of developing dedication to the defined values through interpreting and assessing commitment to them. Based on the work of values clarification guru Dr. Sidney Simon et al. (1995), we ask three important questions:

- Is this value freely chosen? (Do I really own it?)
- Is this value prized and cherished? (Do I really care about it?)
- Is this value publicly affirmed and acted upon? (Do I really "live it" in my everyday activity?)

The process for fully developing and integrating organizational values is shown on the following chart: stage 1 is all about "codifying the values"; stage 2 then moves on to take these codified (stated) values into both who and how we hire and how an organization develops its leadership talent; stage 3 focuses on actually doing business in a way that reflects those values (e.g., building relationships between employees as well as with suppliers and customers); and finally, stage 4 is all about developing a feedback system that allows objective assessment of "what we say is what we do."

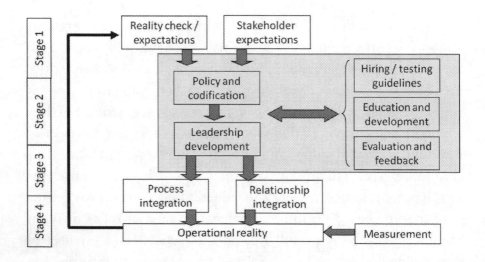

The bottom line is that you cannot pay lip service to values; otherwise it's essentially a waste of time and effort. So we need personal commitment from the top down. Obviously a key tool for assessing whether these statements are true is needed in the form of some type of ongoing survey instrument, which we also develop as part of the process (see "Values Evaluation and Assessment" as a template at the end of the book).

Another key activity that leaders need to engage in when developing organizational values is the concept of "Is/Is Not"; we have found this very effective in developing a real understanding of what a typical sound-bite-sized value statement says and what it really means. As an example, we were working with the board of directors of a private company, all of whom were also executives holding leadership positions, and we developed a series of values statements. This experience is written up more fully in one of our case examples (see chapter 9), but in this particular situation, we had a value that read, "We are committed to being environmentally responsible." That sounds clear enough, right? Well, not really, because when we started discussing what sort of decision making would reinforce this value and what would detract from it, the responses varied widely. We asked one of the directors to tell us in his words what he thought it meant. His response was, "Being environmentally responsible means ensuring that we adhere to the legislation, rules, and standards that exist within all of the operating environments that we have facilities in and that we experience no deviations."

Before we could respond, another director jumped in and indicated that he thought that was "an irresponsible interpretation" because their company, which was a world leader in the work that it did, was well aware of what the leading-edge environmental practices were in the most controlled areas that they worked in and that they should be implementing these leading-edge practices wherever they were operating in the world. A very different interpretation of what this value really meant in practice!

Without this discussion, what guidance would the board and the senior executives be using as a benchmark against which to evaluate and assess capital investment requirements for new equipment? This is typically how values go astray: we all make assumptions that we understand what they mean, and we all know the problem with making assumptions! The "Is/Is Not" tool becomes a very important step in moving toward a better understanding of what values really are all about from an operational perspective.

Stage 2 embeds the commitment into the organizational fabric; this involves permeating the commitment across the whole enterprise (it does not mean "sending out an e-mail" or a "tweet"). People only really start to buy in to organizational values when they understand what they mean in their own reality (i.e., in the job that they do on a day-to-day basis). This means that the organizational values have to be discussed and cascaded down through the organization in a forum that allows discussion and debate. This process is extremely valuable, as it will show up again in situations where there is significant misalignment between what is being said about values and what actually happens in real life ("See that plaque on the wall that lists our corporate values? Great, isn't it? But that's not *really* what we do here!"). We often support the development of "sub values" statements within the working environment, because if a department can take the high-level organizational values and then discuss them in the terms of their own day-to-day activity, then it can develop a set of departmental values that are aligned with, but a subset of, the organization's values.

This second phase is also where we start ensuring that the values are embedded in key elements of the human design of the business. This means that values must be assessed as part of selecting and hiring staff and in the orientation, training, and development of every employee, especially in the area of leadership development. Employee evaluation must also be aligned with the values system so that tools such as 360-degree feedback approaches assess the individual's value system based on observation and interaction with others.

Stage 3 takes this embedding one step further and ensures that in addition to policy and human resource management alignment, processes are also aligned. What does this mean? A simple example would be an organization that indicates that its priority is building effective relationships yet fails to involve key customers or suppliers in its own business strategy, including product and service design. A good example of an organization that appeared not to succeed in this was GM. The automaker had an adversarial approach to vendor-relationship management, yet in the same competitive business, Toyota's approach was equally focused on cost reduction, and it appeared to succeed. To succeed, the organization starts to align its task aspects of mission, vision, and objectives (i.e., the tangible outcomes of the business strategy) with the values that deal with the behavioral aspects of how these outcomes will be achieved. The graphic illustrates this alignment:

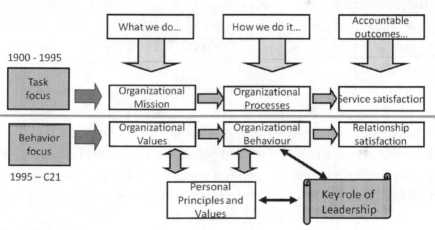

Shepherd / Eduvision © 2007

In today's knowledge economy, where the effectiveness of human interaction creates an intangible asset that contributes to both organizational value as well as competitive advantage, a management framework that embraces the combination of task (what we do) and behavior (how we do it) has become foundational for success, as the graphic shows, particularly in service organizations, where success is based on "How I was treated" as much as whether "I received what I wanted."

Groundbreaking research conducted on behalf of the Institute of Citizen-Centered Service[15] (ICCS) has demonstrated that in enhancing citizens' satisfaction with public sector services, the role of staff in being knowledgeable as well as how they treated citizens (e.g., "went the extra mile") are cited as one of the top five key drivers of satisfaction. So stage 3 addresses both process activity from embedding into task as well as relationship activity that would deal with how organizational values form a foundational aspect of key stakeholder's dealings. An important aspect of linkage here is that we often work with a board of directors in developing organizational vision and mission and complement this with organizational values that link directly back to the activity of effective stakeholder identification (e.g., Who are they? What outcomes do they expect from use? What behavioral relationship do they expect from us?). Values, therefore, become foundational.

Finally, stage 4 is about closing the loop to ensure that "what we say is actually what we are doing." One of the key sources of failure in making values real is the fact that there is minimal linkage back to any performance management system. It is interesting to note how many corporate scandals can be traced back to behavioral problems rather than process failures. Nick discussed this at some length in his book on corporate governance for the twenty-first century[16]; in an agile, flexible, and fast-moving knowledge economy, internal controls must balance the need for risk taking with an adequate level of control. In this economy, excessive controls create a bureaucracy that gets in the way of the strategic imperatives and decision making of an organization, thus being confident that our people know the behavioral expectations and

---

[15] The mandate of ICCS, based in Toronto, is developing and disseminating leading practices in global public sector "leading practice" management.

we can trust them becomes a key success factor for building an effective twenty-first-century organization. In chapter 7, where we discuss integrating task and relationship activity, we will explore the issue of internal controls in more depth.

In two of the other case studies that we include in this book, we worked with a mining company as well as a business that develops joint ventures with its key customers. We discuss how critical defined and understood values really are. In each of these cases, the values were applied relative to external stakeholder relationships. In one case, the mining organization was dealing with a native community that owned the surface and subsurface rights to where gold deposits had been located and where a mine would be established. In this case, treating these "partners" consistently was absolutely essential in order to create trust. In the other example, a joint venture had been in place over twenty-five years, but during this time, the directors of the company had rotated on and off the board, so "corporate memory" had been lost and the whole foundation upon which the joint venture had been established was becoming forgotten. In this case, a new "director orientation" program was needed to get new directors up to speed quicker; in addition, this also enhanced the identification of new directors being nominated by each partner, as they could now codify what their expectations were of the type of individual who could function effectively on the board.

We have come across many examples where organizations "get it" and have already proceeded down this path. One example is Bruce Power, which operates a large nuclear power generation facility on the shores of Lake Huron. This company is in partnership with Cameco Corporation, TransCanada Corporation, and BPC Generation Infrastructure Trust, a trust established by the Ontario Municipal Employees Retirement System, the Power Workers'

Union, and the Society of Energy Professionals. The organization took over the operation of this plant from the provincial electric utility, which had a history of high operating costs, deficits, capital overruns, and new capacity delays in construction. One of the key areas of focus that the company has developed is its commitment to the community (see the "Company Values and Vision" on its website at www.brucepower.com through which it ensures a constant dialogue with the local community):

"A COMMUNITY-MINDED COMPANY
As the biggest business in our small corner of Ontario, Bruce Power's corporate social responsibility runs deep. We are plugged directly into the social and economic fabric of the communities that surround and support us.
Each year, we enhance the medical, educational, and cultural strengths of our communities through a vibrant sponsorship program that demonstrates our belief that corporate citizenship is central to our ultimate success. To learn more about our guidelines and apply for support, please check out our sponsorship pages".

Why? Is it purely idealistic and philanthropic? Well maybe, but there is a solid business practicality for building these relationships, and that kicks in when problems or issues arise and when changes to the business are taking place—the company already has the contacts and has built the communications network and the trust. Its values statements clearly define those beliefs that are to guide its business actions.

As indicated earlier, we also use a similar approach with boards of directors whose role is to provide organizational oversight and direction. In today's environment, especially relative to statutory compliance with legislation such as Sarbanes-Oxley (SOX), it is critical that behavioral expectations come from the top. In our work with boards, these interventions involve ensuring that the board understands the concepts of corporate governance and the accountability and responsibility that go with that. Then we help the board define who their stakeholders are, and from there, we move on to developing the mission, vision, and values statements necessary to establish direction for the organization. In the next chapter, we discuss the importance of leadership within an organization in actually deploying the values and building the relationships.

At the board level, the critical issue is ensuring that the linchpin that links the board to the day-to-day management of the business (e.g., the CEO or executive director) is selected on the basis of alignment with the defined values of the organization. If this fails to happen, boards should not be surprised when the practical activities start to go astray from what they expected would happen.

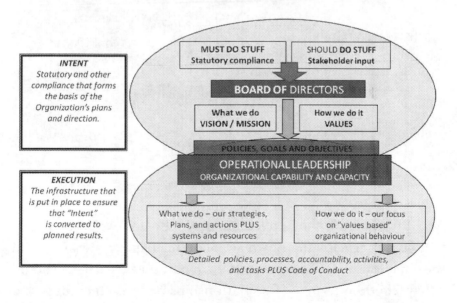

This schematic shows how the operational leadership position plays such a key role in effective governance in linking the expectations and intent of the board into day-to-day actions.

As can be seen, expectations typically fall into two categories: mandatory compliance areas and discretionary expectations.

The next graphic shows an approach that we suggest organizations take in developing these two sets of expectations and how these then form the basis for the way in which the organization is managed (the management model). While this book is not intended as a focus on corporate governance, the importance of effective definition of organizational values must really start at this level.

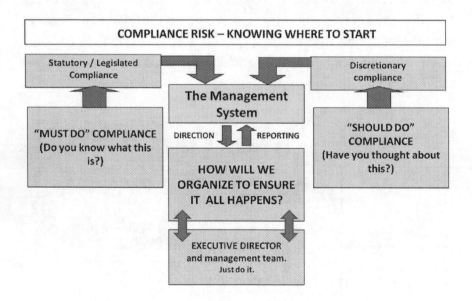

As a final note on the application at the board level, we suggest that boards develop their own set of performance criteria around the organizational values, as applied to how the board itself should behave, both in terms of its relationships between members and also with external stakeholders and with management. This not only helps clarify the values in practical terms for the board but allows the board to establish a set of performance criteria against which the board can self-assess its performance on an annual basis. We often hear of boards wanting to create a self-assessment program for improvement, but we also have found that when we ask, "What will you be assessing yourself against?" there is not really a well-defined answer.

CHAPTER 5

LEADERSHIP AND A VALUES-BASED

ORGANIZATION

The I that I know does not know enough to know
that it does not know enough!
James Hollis

Leadership and the Integration of Values

In an increasingly alienated and stressed-out world, the need for clarity of values has become ever more important. As suggested earlier, many leaders merely pay lip-service to their stated values or say that they simply don't have the time to think about issues relating to values; they're just "too busy." The apparent disconnect between words and actions has widened, as has the emotional distance between leaders and their people (as well as people-to-people). Much of this is happening outside of the conscious awareness of the leaders themselves. Of course, many would deny this, saying that they know themselves well enough (as we all do!). Developing consciousness, therefore, becomes a major challenge of leadership. Leaders who are grounded in the here-and-now and have a good sense of the thoughts, feelings,

60

aspirations, and motivations of those around them are empowered to adjust and adapt to the requirements not only of the situation at hand, but also to the personal and interpersonal requirements of self and others. So ultimately, the goal is a conscious awareness of the "what" and the "how" of leadership. The *what* refers to the task to be achieved; the *how* refers to relationships and working with others. This constitutes what we refer to as "reflective leadership."

In essence, the greatest gift leaders can give to themselves is *consciousness*. This implies the ability to be consciously *responding* to the world and its demands, as opposed to *reacting*. Being responsive puts you in the driver's seat; being reactive puts you at the mercy of the vehicle itself—and indeed other vehicles on the road! The difference is the distinction between slavery and freedom; between *having feelings* and the *feelings having you!* Values act as guides to decisions and actions. The internalization of values through thought and consistent action creates the framework for values-based leadership. This implies an internal dialogue that considers the complexity of problem solving and decision making—but from a perspective of defined values.

Congruence between values and actions results in a sense of integrity. This is the *leadership challenge*! True leaders operate from a position of principle: a clear code based on a conscious set of fundamental ethical truths that guide their conduct. Leadership competencies are strengthened to the extent that the leader's attitudes and behaviors correspond to these articulated principles.

Why do we say "articulated"? Because they are declared! If values are founded on fundamental principles, and if an important aspect of the values-clarification process is the public affirmation of these principles and values, then the individual leader is strengthened to the degree that these are both declared and lived. In essence, it takes both integrity and courage to be an effective leader. This is often referred to as the "character" of leadership, in particular as discussed by Alexandre Havard[16] (Havard, 2007). There is little or no dissonance between what is articulated and what is acted upon.

If we accept the link between values and integrity, then the conscious leader manifests values through action. This is the process of not only leadership development, but organizational development too. The strength of the organization is in proportion to the strength of the leader(s) of the organization. The power of Praxis[17] resides in the articulation (based on understanding) and the manifestation (based on action) of values. This is also the essence of true empowerment.

So why doesn't every leader simply adhere to a set of principles and values? This is a complicated question with multiple and equally complex answers. Individual histories, beliefs, motivations, and intentions provide but part of the answer. We believe that narcissism provides another important part.

Leadership and Narcissism

Western society has become increasingly narcissistic. Self-absorption has become the order of the day. In our society of individualism, competitiveness, self-entitlement, and acquisitiveness, the "I" has attained standards never before imagined by our more communitarian ancestors. Not that

---

[16] Alexandre Havard. *Virtuous Leadership*. New York: Scepter Publishers. 2007.

[17] The ability to translate an idea into action.

narcissism was recently invented; Aristotle himself made reference to the notion that "we are hopelessly self-absorbed."[18] Imagine if he were to witness the hopelessness of today! The common condition of self-centeredness plagues relationships in every quarter, and no less in the modern business world.

The narcissistic style of many who are in positions of leadership preempts the possibility for others to participate and be truly included in the life of the organization. As the "false self" (living up to some extraneous expectations) of the narcissistic leader shows up in extreme self-involvement, this becomes evident to others, but not to him/herself. This leader is simply "gung ho" and enamored with his/her own thoughts, projects, and activities. Unaware of his/her own cathexis (emotional connection) in relation to desires and wishes, this leader is operating from a base of unconsciousness and is therefore unaware of the impact he/she has on others. The noose of unconsciousness affects not only the bearer but all those in his/her environment. Negative reactivity comes from a lack of awareness of the inner self. In Jungian terms, an overemotional response to a small provocation is an indication that a complex has been ignited. (A "complex" comes from unresolved repressed feelings that, when triggered, often result in reactive and harmful interpersonal behaviors.) So we see that many in positions of leadership are quite complex!

It has been said that self-governance is the highest form of leadership. How we govern or run our own lives is indicative of the level and type of leadership we possess. Leaders who feel integrated (whole) will invariably do better than those who experience an inner sense of disorganization and conflict. Emotionally insecure

---

18   *The Complete Works of Aristotle: The Revised Oxford Translation.* Jonathan Barnes, ed. Princeton, NJ: Princeton University Press. 1984.

leaders will be _too_ certain and demanding of their people. The consequences of this include a hampered and disillusioned workforce. On the other hand, emotionally secure leaders, with a true sense of confidence, will engage others in the achievement of goals and objectives, based on a clearly defined vision, strongly supported by a clear set of values. Evocative leaders bring forth the best in their followers—they _evoke_ emotional and sensory responses that are positive. These leaders have an awareness of their followers' needs for respect, acknowledgment, inclusion, and a sense of control over their respective responsibilities. This becomes a hopeful and empowering place to be. Loyalty is inspired through the development of trust and engagement. This, of course, has powerful implications for the question of employee motivation and retention.

Narcissistic leaders, on the other hand, diminish hope in their followers. These leaders are essentially unaware of their impact on others. Being so task-driven, their only concern is with "outcomes," regardless of the means of achieving them—especially the interpersonal relationship aspects. While conscious leaders give hope, unconscious leaders take it away. Narcissism precludes true respect for others and _their_ reality. Regardless of the pronouncements and motivational work-ups of narcissistic leaders, they will not develop true "followership," just obedience and conformity—which, of course, are rewarded! Leadership without integrity is like a well without water! If the "_Me_" is bigger than the "_We_," then problems, often with an unspecified and arbitrary source, will erupt, leaving people feeling unmotivated and disheartened.

If one adheres to the concept of German philosopher Martin Buber's I-Thou relationship, a respectful relationship between equals, then it becomes apparent that the _power over_ model is antithetical to the more humanistic notion of the *power with* model fostered by those who practice leadership based upon consciousness and lived values.

Does this mean that narcissistic leaders cannot have values? Of course not! However, when one's values exist within a paradigm of self-centeredness and power-over, then the energy of the bearer of such values will only be maintained by a self-serving and grandiose perspective. And this represents a major problem in today's leadership, where the *power paradigm* prevails and where a devotion to "winning at all costs" costs so much. This calls for a return to an ethical view of leadership—one founded on principles that move beyond idiosyncratic notions and mere individual opinions and preferences. Reason, when combined with passion, makes for a potent balance between task and relationship. Evidence-based leadership considers the psychosocial, cultural, and historical aspects of the job of true leadership.

Values provide a more holistic approach to leadership. Typically, values will relate to three major human traits: *thinking, feeling,* and *wanting.* The logical and the emotional will always play a part in all of our endeavors, and given that we can never arrive at perfection in either of these attributes, we are therefore always in the process of personal development. The overuse of thinking, feeling, or desiring creates an imbalance. However, values-based leadership regards all three as critical in the intentional and purposeful activities of meaningful and effective outcomes.

The Values-Based Leader

Values-based leaders understand that if their organization does not have a set of integrated values, then everything is negotiable! Values guide thinking and behaving. While this may sound simple, we have experienced that developing a truly successful and integrated values-based organizational culture requires three to five years. Why? Because the process of planning, engaging, clarifying, interpreting, integrating, following up, and reviewing takes time. In addition, as an organic and ongoing process, it is under regular review in so far as the set of stated values is used as a benchmark for all important decisions, directions, and actions. At the turn of the century, William James, the father of psychology in North America, commented, "My experience is that which I agree to attend to." Attention to values ensures that they will intentionally influence our experiences. This is what we want: the realization of values through the lived experience of them.

In our terms, values provide a roadmap to success. Our corporate clients tell us of the demanding nature of this process, *but also of its value*! Holding oneself accountable to a set of values and being held accountable by others has the impact of strengthening not only the individual, but also the organization. If leadership is the art of managing the unmanageable, then values provide a framework for this difficult proposition. Subjectivity (taking things personally) is diminished as objectivity (rational emotional detachment) increases through the guidance provided by clarified values. This assists the leader to be less impulsive and more deliberate in responding to difficult demands. "Reason over passion" may be the conscious leader's mantra! This is not to suggest a reduction in enthusiasm but rather a movement from egocentric thinking to rational thinking, as guided by values.

Egocentric leaders are self-centered and guided by the smog of narcissistic thinking. They are led by their own self-serving interests; all of their energy is focused on the validation of their own goals and projects. These leaders do not evoke trust, as they are overly identified with success (task) to the detriment of their affiliation (relationship) with others. To them, the end justifies the means. Though intelligent and often successful, they are frequently seen as unreasonable, manipulative, and often unscrupulous in their dealings with employees and even customers. They are known for being defensive, irritable, and arrogant. They lack true empathy, a key aspect of narcissism; their sensitivity to others relates only to themselves. The *other(s)* becomes *them*, and they are objectified and regarded only in terms of their perceived utility. The objectification of others has become a major source of disconnection and alienation in the workplace of today.

Sigmund Freud referred to the *narcissism of small differences.*[19] While they may intellectually wish to get along with others, egocentric leaders will demonstrate a hostile attitude toward *any* disagreements or critique of their pronouncements or projects. Conformity is rewarded and disobedience punished. Essentially, people learn to simply shut up and obey. Bereft of humanistic values, workplace morale is predictably low, and employee motivation is influenced by a desire to be somewhere else.

Humanistic leaders, on the other hand, are other-centered and guided by a belief in the intrinsic worth and dignity of self and others. To them, the core is the self. These leaders are rational and attempt to see things as they are; they have the capacity to engage others respectfully with a genuine and compassionate concern for their needs and with an active appreciation for their contributions and aspirations. They understand that the workplace is more than a place to make a living. Rather, it is a place for the enhancement of self-respect and self-actualization, regardless of the nature of the business. They are resonant, evoking strong emotions in their

---

[19]   Sigmund Freud. *Civilization and Its Discontents.* New York: W. W. Norton. 1989.

followers, who develop a willingness to go beyond the extra mile. Humanistic leaders are conscious leaders. Their demeanor is characterized by the acquisition of knowledge and a commitment to ongoing learning and development. They invite doubt and are not thrown off by questioning and skepticism; they want to respond to the uncertainties and ambivalences presented to them.

They are fair-minded and sometimes tough—as required by the demands of the situation. Being informed by their own internalized values as well as those of the organization, they will be known for their willingness to take a stand in light of any transgression of values. People are held to account, but they trust their leader and know that they will be treated fairly. These leaders inspire positive energy, motivation, and a committed followership. They have humor and understand the importance of irony and paradox. Few things are of life-and-death importance, but they take serious matters seriously and make distinctions between what is and what isn't.

Humanistic leaders can appreciate the words of James Hollis (2008): *"The I that I know does not know enough to know that it does not know enough."* They are seekers of truth and wisdom, and incorporate this search into their daily activities. When things go wrong, they investigate the reasons and engage others in the exploratory process, never losing sight of the desired balance between the task and the relationship that is necessary for a successful resolution. Their aspiration to achieve this balance is manifested in how they constantly think about the *team.* They know that inclusion, not exclusion, is the key to survival and success. They also know that leadership is not about *being* (a leader), it's about *doing.* Action is their call, and their aim is to create conscious teams that vigorously buy into the task-relationship (T-R) paradigm.

Leadership and Dissonance

> *Knowing is not enough; we must apply.*
> *Willing is not enough; we must do.*
> Goethe

While few leaders would deny the importance of the task-relationship balance, there is sufficient evidence that the effective attainment and maintenance of this equilibrium is the exception and not the rule. There is frequently an obvious gap (dissonance) between what one says and what one does, which creates conflict for all concerned.

If the center of values-based leadership is values-in-action, dissonance (or discordance) occurs whenever the stated values are not being lived in a consistent and predictable manner. This has important implications for the question of trust and integrity. If a leader's behavior is not in accord with stated values/philosophy, then that person's leadership is lacking.

In our everyday lives, we are surrounded by examples of dissonance: the parent who insists that his children not lie but tells them to inform a dinner-time caller that he is not home; the manager who insists that others be punctual for meetings but is habitually late himself; the CEO who demands loyalty but is disloyal to others in their absence. Simply put, saying one thing and doing another does not inspire trust. Or, as the great Austrian psychiatrist Alfred Adler said, "Trust only action"!

Dissonant leaders may be impulsive or inflexible. They are either swayed by the demands and moods of the moment or else rigidly fixated on outcomes. Not known for their sense of balance, they are not consciously guided by values and may be easily thrown off track or blinded by their own narrow perspectives. While way beyond the scope of this book, a brief mention of the latest research in neuroscience may help explain dissonance from another perspective.

The so-called *executive function* of the brain, located in the prefrontal cortex (PFC), defines a number of brain processes that are responsible for planning, order, appropriate actions and behavior, staying focused on task, and task completion, as well as carrying through on commitments. Dissonant leaders have serious prefrontal issues; they are not open to feedback, and if they ask for it, they tend not to use it constructively, nor do they tend to learn from their mistakes. Relationships, as stated above, are seen only in terms of their utility; if anything, they are apt to be overly focused on task. But even then, they trip themselves up and perform inconsistently. The "only predictable thing is their unpredictability"—particularly in their dealings with others.[20]

On the other hand, leaders whose executive functions are intact and whose PFCs function properly show consonance between their stated vision, their goals, and their actions. They are centered within themselves and in harmony with their values. They invite others to join them in results orientation, both task or outcome of what is to be achieved, as well as the relationships, or what behavior is expected. This invitation is a sincere summons to engage in a dynamic and respectful process toward successful outcomes. Their level of dissonance is low, thereby increasing the likelihood of employee satisfaction, motivation, and retention. They are prudent and practical in their reasoning as they weigh the consequences of their decisions and actions, incorporating

---

[20] Ancient Chinese proverb, also from movie *Ratatouille*, Disney/ Pixar (2007).

their vision and values into every equation. This is not to suggest that they are aiming for sainthood, but rather that they have a conscious and intentional desire to build effectiveness by reducing dissonance. These leaders build teams that are based on trust—the essential ingredient in a successful T-R balance.

Leadership and Team Effectiveness

> *I am able to control that which I am aware of.*
> *That which I am unaware of controls me.*
> John Whitmore

As indicated above, effective team leaders take a purposeful perspective at all times, never losing sight of the team's vision and goals. They know that team identity is fundamental to team effectiveness. This is based on clarity of team purpose, vision, goals, roles, and responsibilities. As the team is greater than the sum of its parts, it establishes an identity as a unique entity. Knowing that the team exists to achieve some interdependent goal, the desire for synergy forms its fundamental operating system.

Team experiences range from the positive stance of being *unforgettable,* to the neutral (and common) stance of being *unremarkable,* to the regrettable stance of being *unforgivable.* Our intention here is to describe how to make your team unforgettable.

We wholeheartedly and earnestly promote the development of the *learning team.* This team develops a keen awareness of its primary task and the corresponding critical nature of relationship development in order to succeed in its endeavors. Each team member becomes an active collaborator in the process of team leadership development. Using exploratory and supportive techniques, team leaders encourage independent and critical thinking on the one hand and validation of each member on the other. Their desire is to build a strong interdependent team where team members listen and respond to each other, forming the basis of communication and collaboration. By means of the Socratic approach, they ask questions—not just to find answers per se, but also to facilitate a process of engagement, learning, team development, and problem solving.

A team does not simply form of its own volition or because the boss says, "We need to be a team"; effective team leaders have an appreciation of the members' uncertainty about becoming part of a team in the first place. They also look at each team member with compassionate understanding; they know that members need what they need: to be respected, accepted, and included in a process that will facilitate their empowerment and ability to contribute and learn. They know that fear is the villain of true team development, and they are also aware of the need to build a nonjudgmental and trusting environment through which the members' contributions and creativity can flourish.

Time is also a factor in team development; effective leaders understand that the critical factor of relationship development takes time. However, they also know that through an understanding of the stages of team development, they can facilitate a process that is purposeful and therefore make the best use of the time available. Operating on the basis of an accepted theory of team development (such as the model we present) sets professional team leaders apart from lay practitioners, who may fly by the seat of their pants.

Professional team leaders have a deep understanding of team process as well as the importance of the power dynamics within the team. Typically, untrained team leaders will either be far too authoritarian and task focused (to the detriment of relationship development) or too relationship focused, possibly laissez faire and individualistic, thereby truncating any possibility of true T-R success in the long term. With the high demand for achievement in today's business world, the autocratic approach seems to take precedence. However, professional or trained team leaders will be much more likely to take a balanced perspective in facilitating a process toward success.

These leaders are also cognizant of the fact that a group of great individuals does not necessarily result in a great team. While people who are both technically and socially competent are typically required to form a successful team, there is no guarantee that *this* particular collection of individuals will automatically meet the requirements of team effectiveness. To increase the likelihood of team success, conscious leaders will benefit from a usable framework to guide their behavior in facilitating the development of a high-performing team. The movement from being a collection of individuals working on a task to becoming a team will be inspired by leaders who are clear about their philosophical stance as well as understand the requirements for developing a true team.

We know that the higher the degree of leader dominance (autocratic/individualism), the lower the level of team cohesion and effectiveness; the lower the level of leader dominance (democratic/inclusionary), the higher the level of team cohesion and effectiveness. In the former case, the leader *tells*; in the latter, the leader *facilitates*.

If the general cultural expectation is that leaders must be in control of (exert power over) their team, then the likelihood of dominance is greater than if there is an awareness of the desirability of a culture of collaboration (share power with) the team.

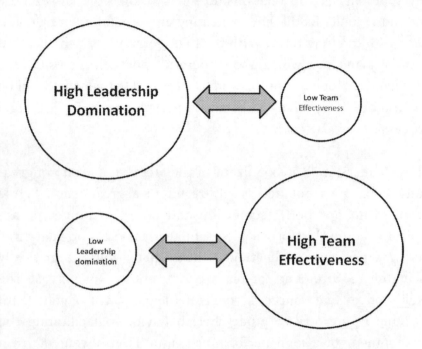

Many have balked at this notion, as the prevalent concept is one of the leaders being in charge. Well, if simply being in charge worked, teams would work—and we'd be out of business! There are exceptions to every rule, and this is not to deny the reality of intuitive, charismatic, and often dominant though effective team leadership, but this is more the exception, and even then, there is usually a passionate buy-in of the leader's vision. Also, the followers admire the leader and feel strongly respected and included.

The Team Shamrock

Although a group of great people does not necessarily make a great team, conscious leaders aim to create a healthy team through a set of "Cs": the facilitation of a process of communication, collaboration, and coordination toward a strong level of commitment to the team's tasks as well as the commitment of each member to one another. According to legend, Ireland's St. Patrick used the shamrock (the three leaves supported by a single stem) to explain the concept of the Trinity to the king of Tara. We use this simple yet iconic symbol as a metaphor for effective team functioning; we call it the *Team Shamrock*.

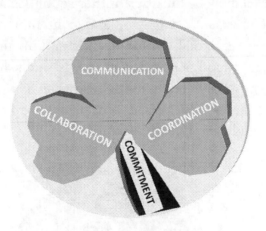

The shamrock is presented to the team as an uncomplicated guide for effective team functioning. This can be easily discussed and used as a framework for development. Early in the life of the team, the leader explains the concept of the shamrock and how it will be used as one of a number of guides to gauge the team's progress, particularly from an interpersonal perspective. Through discussion and by using a simple 0–5 Likert scale, the team begins to become consciously self-reflective.

A positive team culture is enhanced to the extent that the team members perceive that they are developing a *caring community.* While to some this may sound weak, the very essence of social support comes from caring. Caring, rather than being simply a "feeling," is always accompanied by *understanding* and *action.* In other words, it is often very difficult to really care. It requires being other-centered and compassionate, challenging, and supportive. So, the healthy team develops a strong and healthy shamrock to the extent that members learn to care about not only the team's purpose and activities (T), but also each other (R).

The leader also orients the team to the fact that the integrity of the Team Shamrock may be hurt by another set of "Cs": the antiteam behaviors of criticism, cynicism, and contempt. In this case, commitment is replaced by complacency, and the team begins to go to rot! Team mood is low and energy is sluggish at best. The degree of decay doesn't really matter, as when any or all of these characteristics are present, they represent a critical threat to team development and overall team functioning.

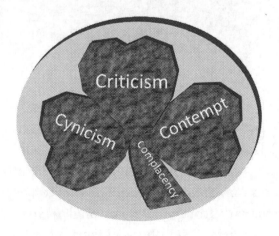

The Underfunctioning Team

In our combined fifty-plus years of experience in working with teams, we have observed that the vast majority of them actually under-function. This, unfortunately, is the norm and is supported by anecdotal and academic evidence. Through the use of simple questionnaires as well as more sophisticated team-effectiveness questionnaires (see the appendix for an example), we have found that the average team, regardless of function or organizational type, scores less than 50 percent in their overall level of effectiveness. The waste in organizational resources (and indeed in human terms) is enormous! Self-reports alone (by team members) strongly suggest that the self-concept of the average team is way below a desirable level. We've had medical teams complain of their underfunctioning and poor morale, and the negative impact this has for patient care. Many manufacturing teams also report high levels of fear, disengagement, and the accompanying negative impact on productivity and quality. As the Big L (Task and Relationship) suffers, so too does the team.

Feelings of disillusionment and personal inadequacy are rampant, and as teams typically do not develop good coping mechanisms, an underlying anxiety prevails for many. Oddly enough, we get what we tolerate, and while there seems to be impatience with the status quo, there is also a begrudging acceptance of "this is just the way it is."

CHAPTER 6

MAKING IT REAL: A RELATIONSHIP-BASED

ORGANIZATION

Leadership and the Values-Based Organization

In the previous chapter, we discussed the importance of the leader in developing a climate where commitment to relationship development is founded on a set of defined and demonstrated values. We also introduced the importance of the leader developing inclusivity in building an organization that shares these values, and we demonstrated the importance of team development as a core element of this strategy.

In this chapter, we further define and develop the steps involved in building an effective team. While this must start at the leadership level within any organization, the principles apply to the development of teams at any level and for any purpose within the organization.

The Team as a Challenge for Leadership

A ship is safe in a harbor, but that's not what ships are for.
Anonymous

Clearly, the successful launching of the team becomes a challenge for team leadership. However, rational and effective team leaders will have a conscious and clear awareness of the *what* (T) and the *how* (R). In the team process, progress of the T-R dynamic is discussed and documented. Effective team leaders bring out the very best in people and aim to develop a high-performing team. While they may have an intuitive awareness of the fact that teams tend to go through stages of development, they can be further guided by the utilization of a team-development model to increase their level of effectiveness.

There are many models of group and team development in the literature. A number of these have informed our practice in working with teams, and we have seen their utility in making teams become high-performing. Based on the notion that "If you can name it, you can change it," being able to identify the developmental stage of a particular team gives one the ability to intervene or facilitate appropriately. In developing our own framework for understanding team development, we have relied on our experience as well as the literature to provide guidance in the articulation of what we refer to as the *Core Model of Team Development* (referred to here simply as the Core Model).

This six-stage model provides team leaders with a theoretically and experientially sound framework for understanding team development and their role in relation to each of the stages. This can assist one's practice through the acquisition of a realistic and objective understanding of what's needed to bring the team together toward the development of cohesiveness and effectiveness. While being true to the model itself and its main stages, below is our explanation of it, identifying the stage and the team leader's role in relation to the task-relationship requirements of each stage. Sustainability is an important factor for many team initiatives, but it is often overlooked; the investment in a team should be sustainable. The final stages in our model differ from many others in that the goal of sustainability is part of the process, as are the steps toward achieving it.

Furthermore, what is presented here is a closed-membership team, meaning that the members have been selected based primarily on their content knowledge or job-related skills, with the intention of working together over a period of time toward the achievement of some identified goal(s). This may apply to an ongoing senior management team, a department team, or a project team that meets over a period of time. While many teams are of an ad hoc and often brief nature, the model still applies. Does the duration of the team impact team effectiveness? We have found that while duration is certainly a factor in team development, many teams, despite meeting for extended periods of time, never achieve true team success, while short-term teams with a specific focus may indeed meet the developmental criteria for effectiveness.

Effective organizations (including effective teams) are developed from a collection of individuals who come together, and function cooperatively and collaboratively, to succeed in achieving a common purpose.

The Core Model of Team Development

Despite the variability of the many models of team development, many of these models refer to three distinct stages: (1) beginning, (2) middle, and (3) ending. The Core Model also incorporates these three main stages, with each containing two primary substages, making for a six-stage model. The beginning stage consists of the *Formation* and *Deliberation* stages; the middle stage consists of *Amalgamation* and *Consolidation*; the ending stage consists of *Summation* and *Evaluation*.

We refer to our teamwork paradigm as the Core Model, because at its core is a deep respect for the dignity, worth, and integrity of each team member, as well as for the unfolding process of the team itself. There is a clear understanding of the inherent human need for belonging, control, and responsive relationships. The ubiquitous objectification of the person is replaced by an acceptance of the person as subject (vs. object). Few would deny that respect is a critical interpersonal requirement in all of our relationships. (What organization does not hold this as a stated core value?) However, in reality, the lack of respect is one of the main complaints of so many in the workplace today—along with the attendant negative consequences for the organization. From a humanistic perspective, the Core Model holds the value of the person as the ultimate value, and this orients the behavior and attitudes of the team leader in a way that supports the principles of respecting, caring, understanding, and responsibility. While this may sound easy and akin to "motherhood," the application of these principles may be very difficult if one has not internalized the appropriate and corresponding values. Awareness of the values is the first step in the process of deciding whether one sees the importance of such a set of guiding principles.

Stage 1: Formation

> *I refuse to join any club that would have me as a member!*
> Groucho Marx

The team "begins" before it actually begins! With a new team, preteam activity, including identification of need, definition of purpose, and membership criteria, all take place before the team's first meeting; the better the planning, the better the team and its outputs. We refer to this essential aspect of the Formation stage as the *preteam phase.* From a leadership perspective, and ultimately from the perspective of a successful team outcome, there is no substitute for proper planning and preparation.

Once the team meets for the first time, it enters an initial discovery period, when the new members come together and feel out the prospect of becoming a team. The main theme here is the development of a sense of purpose and inclusion, but this is typically hampered by a sense of "approach-avoidance"—ambivalence toward becoming involved. This is the stage of pre-affiliation, which is often characterized by ambiguity and uncertainty. A level of anxiety or uneasiness may be present as members attempt to understand the requirements of the team task and who they are in relation to the other members—the relationships. Also, questions of "Who's in charge?" and "How will I fit in?" tend to be uppermost in participants' minds. Although the members may have already worked together on other projects and even on other teams, the coming together of *this* team for *this* purpose represents the development of a new entity and a new opportunity.

There are pros and cons involved in teams with members who have had prior experience with each other. The pros include familiarity with and awareness of each other's style. The cons include familiarity with and awareness of each other's style! As human beings, we develop perceptions of others—many of which become fixed in our minds, thereby placing limitations on the potential for openness to further, unknown aspects of other people and their thoughts, feelings, personality, and skills. Additionally, as there is no "neutral" in the emotional life of the person, we have feelings and reactions to all others and to all events that we perceive and experience. Much of the time, this process is outside our conscious awareness. So we can take it as a given that while we may fear strangers, we may also carry baggage about others we have known before.

Whatever the makeup of the team, leaders can facilitate a successful formation phase by being clear about the team's purpose, goals, and objectives. In this period of team construction, they are committed to the philosophy of democratic participation and respect that individuals participate in their own unique way. They know that on one hand, members need to understand their roles and responsibilities within the team; on the other hand, they seek similarity and mutuality in relation to each other. Typically, in a bid for inclusion and acceptance, new members tend to be nice to each other in this beginning phase. Initial commitments are being explored, but with appropriate caution—especially if the team is a new one, or if, as mentioned above, the members already have fixed notions of each other due to having worked together in the past.

We once heard about a leader who had initially supported team development but who later said, "We are committed to building a team; nobody leaves this room until I see some team behavior!" This is not quite the process we have in mind, nor does it deliver the necessary message of commitment. As we often say, team development is *not* like baptism—"one dip and you're done"!

Facilitating by asking questions and building on commonality helps to reduce tension and increase buy-in. A discussion aimed at exploring the members' positive and negative past team experiences helps to set the stage for deciding how we'd like *this* team to be. With an awareness of one's natural need for inclusion and acceptance, effective leaders acknowledge each member's presence and encourage contributions, responses, and linkages: "What do others think about what John just said?" "Have others had a similar experience?" and so on.

The development of a *team vision statement* needs to occur early in the life of the newly appointed team. While the sponsoring organization may itself have a vision statement, the new team needs to develop its own, within the context of the organization's. The same applies to the development of a set of shared values for the team—these will also be constructed within the framework of the organization's set of declared values. However, both vision and values will belong to the team and will act as its beacon for all future activities—statements against which the team will measure all of its directions, decisions, and performance.

What we are describing here is a *living* vision founded upon a set of *living* values. In our experience, although many teams develop statements of vision and values, these are often regarded as an "exercise" without much functionality. Very few teams are able to describe, with any degree of accuracy, their vision and values. So they become inert documents based upon a mechanistic procedure, resulting in later disillusionment and frustration.

As an example, former Ford CEO Donald Peterson discussed how the automaker focused on its human development aspects as part of its quality drive in the 1970s;[21] as CEO, Peterson committed to quarterly "town hall" meetings at which employees could ask questions and participate in discussions about the business. The financial community was aghast at this idea, saying that "spending this much nonproductive time would result in a massive loss of unabsorbed overheads."[22] Peterson's reply was that to *not* have these meetings would cost the company far more in the long term. That's the message: this approach is a long-term cultural commitment based on values. (For more on this approach, look no further than the foundation of the Toyota Management System,[23] where the cultural commitment at the board level provides the foundation to "the Toyota Way.")

For most types of teams, there exists what humanistic group work theorist Norman Goroff refers to as the *external push*:

---

[21] Ford Motor Company, 1970s.

[22] Peterson, Donald E. (1991) *A Better Way*: Houghton Mifflin

[23] Jeffrey Likert. *The Toyota Way*. New York: McGraw-Hill. See also *Toyota Culture* by the same author.

an external demand for a group of people, working together, to successfully complete a task or tasks. Not everyone willingly tap-dances into the team! This presents leaders with one of their main challenges—to move the team from the *external push* to an *internal pull,* facilitating the creation of an environment where members embrace the notion of the team, its tasks, and in due course, each other. Feeling that *there is something here for me* and *that I can make a contribution,* members begin the process of moving from "me" to "we." A sense of ownership is central to team effectiveness. This provides the team with positive energy. Energy gives power: the power to do, to resolve, to stabilize, and to succeed in the overall team endeavor. Energy supplies the team with the motivation to translate its understanding of its purpose into action. Possessing a clearly defined and agreed-upon rationale gives the team a sense of intentionality and meaning. As Paul Tillich observed, a sense of meaning is the "ultimate concern." Without this, we tend to lack energy and motivation and simply go through the motions. This, of course, results in a sense of personal and interpersonal disconnection ("What are we doing here?") and alienation for team members. The result is the diminishment of each team member's sense of self as well as a lack of confidence in the team itself.

Just as Dr. Carl Jung suggested that the goal of the developing self is wholeness, so too, in our view, is the goal of the developing team. Team self-definition is a critical factor in the process of team development. This unique entity, which we refer to as the team, contains many of the elements of personality, as does the individual personal entity of the self. This also suggests that the team is vulnerable to internal conflicts and external demands. What is going on for the team member is concurrently going on for the team, and vice versa. Knowing this assists leaders in their quest to facilitate a process that will move a disparate collection of individuals into a cohesive unit. The quality of the Formation stage is therefore fundamental to the question of whether we will become a team at all!

As *attendance* at team meetings is a critical aspect of team development and success, leaders must make this a clear expectation in the first meeting and ask for a clear commitment to the team. If anything is counter to the team's growth, it is the detrimental effect of inconsistent and poor attendance. Basic to commitment is simply *showing up*. The team must take priority on each member's calendar. Of course, things happen and members sometimes cannot attend for good reason, but in the interests of the developing organism, the component parts must be present! While acknowledging the importance of having cross-functional representation of various roles within the organization, it is better to have a team of four committed people than a team of eight people in which commitment is lacking by one or more members. Often smaller is better!

Stage 2: Deliberation

As active participation increases at this stage, members begin to express their views and positions on emerging issues. Characterized by the question of finding one's place in the team, team members begin to move from a tentative position to a more vocal one in an attempt to define issues relating to the question of power, control, and status within the team. This is usually couched in matters pertaining to content around purpose and goals—a more subtle way of declaring one's position and rank in the emerging team. While these questions are being considered, members are also taking into account each other's skill level, how problems are going to be addressed, and how decisions are going to be made. This is when members begin to test each other and attempts are made to define tasks and relationships.

Team hierarchy is an important aspect of this stage. This question affects both T and R, as members define their tasks and how they are going to achieve them with reference to each other. Although interpersonal conflict tends to be subtle and covert, overt conflict may begin to emerge and show up in the form of tense disagreements. With some teams, one-upmanship is quite apparent as members attempt to claim their status position within the team. However, it is important to remember that ownership and inclusion are critical at all times, and certainly no less now.

The leader's role here is to appreciate this stage; although difficult, it is a necessary step in the development of the team. How it is handled will greatly impact how members are going to feel about the team and their experience of it. Being mindful of the fact that members bring their own talents and skills, the leader allows for, and even encourages, the expression of differing opinions. Facilitating a process of communication and negotiation is central to this stage. In consideration of the team's purpose (T), the leader is equally concerned about its process (R). Time needs to be allotted to an ongoing discussion of process at team meetings—preferably in the here-and-now of *what's* happening and *how* it's happening. This is not to suggest an interruption or a hypervigilance in attending to what's going on, but rather an enrichment of the process through thoughtful inquiry and reflection. This facilitates *awareness* for members and contributes to the ongoing development of team trust.

All members are encouraged to participate in deciding direction and in decision making; leaders see their role as influencers and incorporators of all viewpoints, opinions, and contributions.

While autocratic leaders simply push their agenda forward, thereby truncating team development, democratic leaders reach for buy-in, through acknowledgment, explanation, clarification, and questioning. At all times, their questions serve to facilitate the T and the R. This also suggests that inclusion is increased to the extent that what the members *feel* is as important as what they *think.* And while recognizing emerging difficulties and conflicts, they are reminded of the old Irish saying, "'Tis easier to ride a horse in the direction it's going."

Stage 3: Amalgamation

This is the stage when members begin to *feel* like a team. The team is beginning to feel more enlightened, and a sense of cohesion begins to emerge as the team becomes clear about its purpose, shared vision, values, goals, roles, and responsibilities. The closeness develops as members show support for each other and are willing to be more open about their thoughts and feelings—both negative and positive. The interaction, however, is well-intentioned, and participants experience incipient trust and safety. The communication and collaboration functions of the team become stronger, and a sense of team identity begins to emerge. The indicators of team success emerge as the members develop a sense of hopefulness about their team experience.

Effective leaders acknowledge the growing interdependence among the members and affirm this as a sign that the team is moving toward its goals and objectives. By now, they are clearly accepted as collaborators who have the best interests of the team and its purpose at heart. At this stage, difficult team issues are addressed, and the "untalkable" becomes "talkable" as leaders encourage members to be open. Of course, effective leaders model appropriate openness and flexibility. They challenge those actual or perceived obstacles to the accomplishment of the team's purpose (T) as well as any impediments to the team's functioning (R). They use clarification and confrontation to understand those issues that might prevent some tasks from being accomplished. Still, they are seen as strongly empathetic and respectful of every member. While using a problem-solving approach, leaders are mindful of the fact that the team's vision and values provide the main framework for commitment and action. They are also aware that it is in the middle stage of team development (Amalgamation and Consolidation) that most of the real work of the team gets done. So, one of the main goals is to continue to build the team itself. Effective leaders know that without developing and maintaining a fully functioning team, everything else is simply commentary!

Stage 4: Consolidation

At this stage, *we now feel like a true team! We feel united—a force to be reckoned with! We are a dynamo team!* The team has developed real sense of ownership and confidence with potent potential. We are now an interdependent and synergistic team with a solid core. Issues of power and control have been resolved, and mutual support and reciprocity have become a reality of team life. The members feel secure as a team and with each other. Trust has been established regarding both axes of T and R, and there is a strong sense of empowerment. Loyalty to each other has, by now, been well established, as has a corresponding level of trust. Equality is an important aspect of this stage. While members may differ in actual status within the organization, at this phase each feels like an equal and valued contributor in terms of the team itself. Also, there is a distinct differentiation between team members—each person is recognized for their uniqueness and is appreciated for his or her distinctive contribution, personality, personal differences, and oddities. In other words, members have each built *idiosyncratic credit* within the team.

Connection creates balance. The team is now in emotional equilibrium. The members have arrived at a place of "effective dependency," to quote attachment theorist John Bowlby. They are able to turn to each other for emotional support, and this, says relational therapist Sue Johnson, is a sign of strength. We cannot overestimate the importance of a sense of belonging in all of our significant relationships, and the high-functioning team is no exception. It is important to remember that trust creates safety, and a sense of safety allows team members to be themselves and harness their intuitions, creativity, and skills.

At this stage, as with all other stages of the team's development, leaders are consciously aware and protective of the integrity of the team. They know that the positive energy of membership (R) and the forward thrust toward success (T) must be maintained by regularly commenting on and evaluating both aspects of T-R. Rather than becoming too comfortable with success, they keep a deliberate focus on outcomes and continue to challenge the team to greater performance on both T and R. Problem-solving and decision-making processes are by now well established as a team norm while all the while occurring within the framework of vision and values. The team is reality-based, and each meeting is purposeful and clear. As team identity is now strong and unified, its synergistic nature allows for the introduction of new and challenging matters. Having clearly moved from "me" to "we," the team identity suggests that the members are able to level with each other without too much concern for personalization or defensiveness. Although conflict may sometimes occur, it is acknowledged and dealt with. Leaders are therefore able to facilitate a process of ongoing demand and engagement—just as the members are also able to do with each other. The establishment of reciprocity and goodwill has become a precursor for effective problem solving and decision making. The team now fully accepts a *collective responsibility* for team success or failure. It is a fully committed, cohesive, and energized organism.

Stage 5: Summation

It's said that all good things must come to an end. At some point in the team process, either a team member will decide to leave or else the team itself will decide to disband. The exiting of an individual team member may present its own concerns to the team, as the makeup of the entity itself is changing and questions of replacing the member may arise. This particular dynamic needs to be handled carefully, not only in terms of who the new member might be and if he or she will fit into the team, but also how receptive the team is to having a new member. In other words, it's as much up to the team as it is to the new member to create a successful transition. How well the body accepts the new "organ" depends, to some extent, on the organ itself, but in our experience, it's more a function of the team's openness to integrating the new member. Healthy and well-developed teams (those that have reached the Consolidation stage) are more successful at assimilating new members than teams that remain underdeveloped and perhaps stuck in the beginning phases of Formation and Deliberation. A planned orientation and welcoming of the new member will assist the team in not losing too much momentum in its process and continuing focus on the T and R of team life. Developing rituals for both exiting and entering members provides the team with a sense of continuity and predictability. New members enter a secure environment, which will no doubt assist them in dealing with their questions and apprehensions about team Formation and Deliberation.

For executive-level as well as many other long-term types of teams that are a permanent aspect of the organization, Continuation might better describe this fifth stage. In this case, team maintenance and sustainability become the focus of attention. In the ebb and flow of team life, regression to earlier stages of development sometimes becomes a reality to be observed and processed. The entrance of a new member might precipitate some regression, or the team might become stuck on some critical issue or on a values or personality-based conflict. It would seem that all long-term relationships enter what Carl Jung referred to as "the unbearable standstill." The team relationship is no exception. Becoming unstuck requires the recognition of *being* stuck and an identification of the issues in need of resolution, particularly from the T-R perspective. While problem-solving and decision-making tools can be very helpful, there are times when recognition must be given to the *unresolved remnant*—that not all T and R issues can be worked out.

If this applies to a task issue, then the task in question is either beyond the scope of the team and its resources or one of those unmanageable items that must be referred elsewhere (or simply dropped). If the issue is relationship based, then it may be a function of an irresolvable personality conflict, some other interpersonal or team issue, or simply a question of commitment to the team. Whatever the issue on the T-R continuum, as with personal problems in our lives, it is often helpful, if not healthy, to acknowledge the concept of the *unresolved remnant* and move on.

In the case of a team that has achieved its primary purpose, leaders must not become seduced by the lure of continuing for the sake of continuing—after all the team has been through and has accomplished. Summation symbolizes a termination, a separation, an ending. For some members, this may be difficult;

it may (unconsciously) become a representation of the ending of past relationships in their lives. The team has become a place of meaning and success. Strong bonds may have formed between the members, and although they may continue to work together (directly and indirectly) within the organization, the notion of not having the team as an important reference point in their work lives may cause some members discomfort. We have observed that some members deny the fact of the team's termination; others regress to an earlier stage of development. Recapitulation of past and perhaps some unresolved issues may occur, and team members may say that there's more to be done.

As with the beginning stages of development, leaders take a more dominant role and focus on helping the team to maintain its sense of cohesion. They affirm the team's accomplishments and recognize the members' feelings—both positive and negative. Their role as an empathic listener is very important at this stage. In essence, they realize that the team has become a social system made up of people who came together for a specific purpose and who developed a meaningful structure of interaction based on communication, collaboration, and coordination of effort. Their commitment to relationship has become equal to their commitment to task—not something they necessarily set out to do in the first place. But wise leaders know that the team would only truly succeed to the degree that a balance of both T and R would be achieved.

And now it must end. This is not meant to sound morose, as an effective team summation and termination process incorporates a celebration of success as well as an evaluation that looks at implications for the future. This brings us to Evaluation as the final stage of team development.

While much discussion has rested on teams within a working environment, it is useful to think about the application of these approaches to group functionality in the context of constantly transitioning teams. As an example, some of our work has focused at the board level. Board members, especially in not-for-profit organizations, are constantly transitioning in and out, often to the detriment of the task aspects of the board's work. A key application of our approach in working with boards is to enable a far more effective transition of team members, so that the board can operate with a higher level of task momentum.

Stage 6: Evaluation

Tied closely with and on the heels of Summation, the Evaluation stage is a time of examination, study, reflection, and planning for the future. While ongoing evaluation of the team's progress and process is built into our model, this particular stage is designed as a thorough review of the team's purpose, vision, goals, and objectives (task) and to what measurable extent these have been met. Also, the Core Model gives special attention to evaluating the team's active process (relationship). This aspect is more unusual than usual. The general norm is for teams to pay far more attention to their tasks than the dynamics and processes by which the members relate to each other. In fact, some of the research suggests that group and team leaders spend less than 5 percent of their time focusing on matters relating to the dynamics of the group or team as a whole.

We consider this to be like wanting to win the Indianapolis 500, but paying little attention to the race car's engine! The team, with all its interactive components, needs to be oiled and constantly maintained.

This is why many teams never reach Stage 4 (Consolidation), a stage of development when the internal dynamics of the team's process of addressing task and relationship is generally not attended to. This would suggest that the norm is to be overly focused on task at the expense of relationship issues. Overlooking internal relationship concerns leads to the avoidance of interpersonal conflict within the team. This can only result in team dysfunction and a corresponding sense of distance and disenchantment for team members. Our own research of conflict avoidance (Smyth, 2006) shows that less than 5 percent of the general population is willing to actively and positively address issues of an interpersonal nature. (The actual number of those willing to do so is a mere 3.5 percent.) About 10 percent will do so in an aggressive/hostile manner; 15 percent will avoid the issue but will act in a pleasant/friendly manner; over 70 percent will actively avoid but in a disgruntled, passive-aggressive manner.

So essentially, conflict avoidance has become the norm, with all of the attendant and unspecified consequences for team development. This clearly becomes a question of leadership, for both the individual team member and team leaders themselves. While we know that the resolution of interpersonal conflict can act as a *team tonic* and increase team morale, unresolved conflict can act as a demotivator and decrease team morale. When appropriate, it is better to identify an *irresolvable issue,* decide on it, and simply move on; otherwise, the team runs the risk of enduring the *unbearable standstill.* With an ongoing evaluation mentality, team leaders teach the importance of reflection and action, of identifying issues and addressing them.

The stage of Evaluation requires that leaders begin by engaging the team in a process of critical self-reflection. Although this is suggested as an ongoing monitoring process throughout the life of the team, at this ending stage, it is more formal in its summary assessment of purpose, vision, goals, objectives, roles, and responsibilities. As with earlier developmental stages, leaders help the team to evaluate its strength on the T-R continuum. Evaluative questions include the following:

- How do we know we have achieved our goals?
- What are the measurables?
- What remains unfinished, and what can we do/recommend regarding this?
- What difference has the team made to organizational and relationship growth and development?
- What outside feedback have we received about our contribution to the organization?
- What have we learned through this process?
- What has the team *meant* to the members at a personal level?
- What are the implications for future teams?
- What is our legacy?
- Where do we go from here?

The Leader and the "As-If" Team

We have also observed a phenomenon that we have dubbed the "as-if" team. This is based on the work of Polish psychoanalyst Helen Deutsch, in which she described the capacity of certain patients to constantly change their self-perception in accordance with the demands of their experiences. She referred to this as the "as-if" personality. This ability to adapt is based on a need for acceptance but is not founded on a true sense of self or of one's core values. The absence of a core sense of inner cohesion suggests a reactive response to external environmental stimuli in order to please—to be accepted. An artificial type of harmony exists in the *as-if team*, but being all things to all people suggests a fluidity and adaptability that lacks depth. Or, as Kurt Vonnegut suggests, "We are what we pretend to be."

The as-if team lacks a true sense of team identity and is therefore guarded in its sense of true team purpose and direction. It is, in fact, a fictitious team. What we have witnessed with these teams is a great imbalance in the task-relationship dynamic and a sense of disorganization. Although members may refer to themselves as a team, they will typically be overly developed in task; but in this case, the task of ostensibly meeting all external expectations and demands. Any task will do! However, one characteristic of the as-if team is one of avoidance and passivity. Tasks are rarely successfully completed, and relations are essentially superficial and abstract. These "pseudo teams" actually get little done, because nothing is really happening in terms of real task accomplishment. Team purpose, vision, values, goals, and objectives are ill conceived, and therefore the team lacks commitment and direction. Taking the *human dimensions* out of the equation leads to a team that is overly focused on externals, its tasks, with little attention to (or mechanisms for discussing and evaluating) its relationships.

How *authentic* is this type of team? From a humanistic leadership perspective, questions regarding ethics arise. When the team as an entity is not founded on shared values, then too much regard is given to content (T) and too little to process (R), particularly as these relate to personal meanings for the members as well as member-to-member interactions. This team tends to be quite unconscious and reactive—usually a victim of fixed and unexamined perceptions. As a collection of individuals who happen to meet for a common purpose, the tendency is to be task driven without much regard for intrateam relationships and examination of real progress. This type of imbalance is usually very costly, in both business as well as human terms.

In this case, leadership blind spots abound as leaders, often unconsciously, enter into a duplicitous relationship with the members and become increasingly unaware of their contribution to the dysfunction of the team. In the absence of a moral vocabulary, guided by an adherence to stated values, the team lacks conviction in its declared purpose, vision, and values. The longer this self-deception endures, the greater will be the dissonance between declarations and behavior, between principles and productivity. This pathology becomes pervasive, and all involved in the team develop an unspoken sense of inadequacy and hopelessness, just waiting for it to end.

In looking at a range of teams, from medical organizations to manufacturing firms, our research suggests that on a 1–10 scale (10 being high), the average team scores an 8 on task focus and 3 on relationship developments. The work of achieving a balance between these two critical team variables presents itself as a challenge to most teams. However, it is true, as stated above, that the illusion of real teamwork often prevails. Difficult interpersonal issues and conflicts are avoided, and "the team under the team" (what's really happening) becomes the unspoken reality. Sun Tzu speaks directly of the need to confront conflict in our environment—ignoring it or submerging it renders us powerless. Plus, the attendant tension and stress of conflict avoidance makes for a weakened organism, whether that be an individual or a team.

Functioning as an as-if team ultimately reduces motivation and commitment, resulting in a sense of disillusionment for all team members and creating a corresponding sense of cynicism. In the absence of true team leadership and a concomitant model based on an articulated theory or philosophy of teamwork and team development, the as-if team will simply trudge along while experiencing low energy and a sense of disconnection. From an organizational perspective, this can be very costly in both human terms and task effectiveness.

Our experience and research suggests that between 70 and 90 percent of problems in the workplace are of an interpersonal nature — not the job-related competencies of employees. The need to get along is enormous, as is the need to develop the social and emotional skills to do so in an effective manner, thus the current explosion in the popularity of programs relating to emotional intelligence, 360-degree, and personality profiling. While these programs may have the potential to be effective, they are less so if not presented within a defined philosophy that regards the dignity and integrity of each person as being of paramount and primary importance.

This all raises the questions, How can we make it *real*? How can we achieve a balance between task and relationship? How do we develop the courage to make it happen?

Effective team leadership requires, at a personal leadership level, a dedication to reality and an acknowledgment of the uniqueness of each team member's perception. In moving toward a conscious balance of task and relationship, leaders know that the team exists in order to achieve goals through interdependent means. Through the establishment of a *collaborative alliance,* each team member becomes an active collaborator in the process. Rather than sacrificing the development of the team on the altar of unanimous consensus, where agreement is rewarded and disagreement is punished, conscious team leaders encourage dialogue based on doubt and dissent. Conflict is not avoided but encouraged in a developing atmosphere of openness and safety. These leaders know that mutual understanding precedes effective problem solving and decision making, that the quality of team tasks is ultimately related to the quality of team relationships. As opposed to the as-if team, the real team has a strong sense of identity and the concomitant self-esteem and confidence that accompanies this clarity of *knowing who we are and what we stand for.*

Leadership and Change

> *If I cannot change when circumstances demand it,*
> *how can I expect others to?*
> Nelson Mandela

The literature on leadership is awash with notions on change and change management. What we have observed is that little has been written about change in relation to the inner life of team leaders. The simple yet complex question, "Who am *I* in relation to the question of change?" must be answered. Taking the time to reflect on one's own fundamental principles and values helps leaders to become more grounded and centered. In a business environment, where assertiveness and action are demanded, reflection and introspection may be seen as passive and weak. Furthermore, the requirement for *certainty* trumps contemplation and ambiguity. While Descartes promoted the concept of *radical doubt*, our modern business processes are mostly linear, based on the notion that we must barge ahead, to get from here to there in the shortest time possible. So as gung-ho leaders attempt to push their certainty, they run into roadblocks set up by their followers. Frustrated, they do not appreciate the nature of paradox: that the more certain they are about their wonderful brainwave, the more resistant others will be, particularly if they have not been actively included in the process. As the saying goes, there's nothing worse

101

than a good idea—especially someone else's! Or, to quote Walter Bagehot, "One of the greatest pains to human nature is the pain of a new idea."

Leadership is all about change: provoking it, promoting it, and encouraging others to engage wholeheartedly in the change process. However, humanistic and democratic leaders have an empathic style that gives them a keen appreciation of how everyone has a different perception of change, the type of change in question, and how it will impact them. Taking a differential approach to change, they know that the personality and past experiences of each team member will greatly influence their response to proposed changes.

Being aware of their own personal difficulties with change helps leaders to develop empathy for those they intend to influence and engage in the change process. Change, like leadership, is often regarded as an *external* process. Actually, we understand it to be mainly an *internal* one. In explaining the "inward journey of leadership," Dr. Wiley Souba sees leadership as a process of personal transformation, an inner journey of self-discovery. This expedition suggests that leaders know themselves, understand their personal relationship to their position as leader, and authentically live by their values. Through this self-exploratory process, they develop deep empathy and compassion for those they lead. They work with conflict without aggression and appreciate that all change evokes feelings and personalized meanings for those being asked to participate in a change process.

If leadership is essentially an *internal journey*, then the process of leadership effectiveness focuses on the internal as much as the external. Our modern world reinforces externalism: the content of our goals, objectives, and projects is "out there"—something essentially outside of one's self. Internalism, on the other hand, suggests that our activities are in accordance with our dearly held beliefs and values, that we are intimately connected to what we do and how we live. As our activities become an extension of ourselves, there is little room for dissonance and detachment and the concomitant isolation from personal values. Conscious leadership is therefore perceived as a self-expressive act; it is authentic and not at all duplicitous. The practice of principle-centered leadership considers the confluence of task and relationship as a constant, continuous, and ongoing process. Conscious leaders are very much a *part of* this process and not *apart from* it! They live up to their principles and values and therefore know what they stand for. Being conscious of their philosophical stance puts them in the driver's seat, while being able to maneuver through and around obstacles that will inevitably challenge their beliefs and values. Knowing that the locus of control is within, they assume responsibility for themselves and the results they get.

For conscious leaders, change is never simply "out there" but "in here." From an ecological systems perspective, they know that as they influence change, they are also influenced by it. Systems theory helps us to understand the interrelationship of all aspects of a system, that a change in any part of the system changes the whole system. This is why we advocate the 5 Percent *Principle of Change.* Realizing that it is the *nature* of the change and not the *extent* of change that is important, we have observed how even slight modifications can produce significant results. For example, we often discuss the manager who rarely says "Good-morning" to his staff, but begins to do so regularly and finds that the atmosphere in the office somehow becomes lighter. There is a subtle, if not discernible, improvement in morale as workers feel a sense of acknowledgment. This positively impacts the interpersonal energy system of the operation and increases a sense of cohesion.

The same applies to managers who work behind closed doors. By simply leaving the door open, they invite openness. (And to think, if they also say, "Good-morning," the sky's the limit!)

In the 1970s, Dr. John Gottman introduced the concept of the *emotional bank account* (EBA). This is a metaphor for all of the positive and negative exchanges between the participants in a relationship. The strength of a relationship is founded on the amount of positive "deposits" in the EBA. The stronger the EBA, the stronger the level of trust, respect, and openness. The weaker the account, the lower the level of these positive attributes. Dr. Richard Weiss added to this further by introducing the concept of the *positive sentiment override* (PSO) and the *negative sentiment override* (NSO). Both positive and negative sentiments are created in everyday, ordinary interactions. So, if in a relationship there is an essentially positive account, then the participants can withstand, if not accept, some negative responses. They are also less likely to interpret ambiguous or even reactive responses in a negative light and will be more forgiving of actual negative reactions. The PSO sustains positive effects, as there is a fundamental sense of goodwill between the parties. On the other hand, if the EBA has not been attended to sufficiently, then any actual or perceived negative responses are met with defensiveness and disdain. The NSO kicks into place and acts to further deplete the emotional bank account.

Understanding this rather simple concept is critical to understanding the requirements of a positive change process. To ignore it is to ignore reality! Many leaders approach the notion of change as though they were operating from an even playing field. The playing field is rarely even, however, as the prework of relationship building is often insufficient with regard to the human requirements of the change process. The stronger the EBA, the stronger the trust and potential for buy-in as the PSO acts to strengthen the immune system of the relationship, whether that be a one-on-one or team relationship.

In our consulting work with a wide range of organizations, we regularly check into the strength of their existing EBA. Given that the people we deal with are typically intelligent and often accomplished in their field, it is sometimes surprising to discover the fractious and negative nature of their interpersonal and team relationships. While nobody would deny the importance of positive relationships and the need for strong emotional bank accounts, there is often a reluctance to actively pursue and develop positive workplace relationships. "We don't have the time to focus on that" is often the expression we hear as we begin the journey of discovery with our clients. The task is strong, but the relationship is weak! How people *feel* is given low priority in the scheme of things. Yet, this is where they live and what they carry with them on a day-to-day basis.

The concept of *Habeas Emotum*[24] suggests that all team members have the right to freely express their feelings. In the affective/ emotional life of the person, nothing is ever neutral; consciously or not, we have feelings about everything that happens to us and about everything we perceive in our environment. Conscious leaders understand this and therefore explore, with their followers, not just what they *think* about impending changes, but also how they *feel* about these changes and new directions. This responds to the reality of *personalized meaning*: that we assign meaning, in our own unique way, to all that we perceive, and no less so than when the concept of change is introduced to us.

---

[24] Luft, Joseph (1969). *Of Human Interaction*.: National Press; Palo Alto, CA

In relation to the change process, the *purposeful expression of feelings* results when leaders simply ask team members how they feel about the impending change and what it means to them. While the change in question may be inevitable, we know from consulting and clinical experience that being asked, in a genuine manner, about the impact that the change might have tends to have a positive impact. For instance, the doctor who sits with the family of a dying patient and responds to their feelings will have a much better outcome than the physician who avoids any discussion of feelings and meaning. Feeling cared about goes a long way, even when the actual results are inevitably contrary to one's wishes.

In the 1970s, Paul Watzlawick quipped, "A primary paradox of human nature is that people will do *anything* to make their lives better—*except* what they need to do." As human beings, we can all relate to this irony, as we all resist something we need to do.

Effective leaders, as agents of change, need to explore their own exceptions—their own issues around the question of change, both generally and particularly, in relation to past experiences with change. Accepting one's own fears of the uncertain and the unknown likely increases the probability that one can accept the fears that others also possess. And yet, the more we can accept that change is in fact fundamental to the nature of things, the more we will be able to consider change as ongoing and natural. Or as Marcus Aurelius very well expressed, "We shrink from change; yet is there anything that does not come without it?"

Individual responses to change vary, and while some may embrace it, it would seem that the norm is to resist it. This is a very complex matter, and it takes maturity and insight to appreciate the usually sensitive nature of others when required to consider a course of change. Obviously, the greater the level of active involvement in the change process, the greater the level of buy-in and the lower the level of apprehension and anxiety. However, as it is not always possible to engage everyone from the beginning of the process, one must consider the climate that exists in the organization and the degree of trust that has been established at all levels. Trust increases openness, flexibility, and the likelihood of buy-in and success. In low-trust environments, change is met with cynicism, criticism, and contempt.

As we will see in the segment of psychometric assessments in chapter 10, individual typology acts as a major feature in one's perception of, and adaptation to, change. While accepting the true uniqueness of every individual, typological similarity gives us a notion as to how *groups* tend to see change. Understanding this gives us a starting point in preparing to introduce a change.

Even at the best of times and in the best of organizations, change can present a challenge. People are being asked to alter their ways of thinking and doing. Over the years, in our coaching and counseling work, we have seen that merely asking a person to do something different can be a difficult proposition. We all know how hard it is to change *any* pattern—even when the change is perceived as desirable.

To facilitate change processes, conscious leaders make a distinction between "communication" and "dialogue." Many will say that they have *communicated* with their people. This often means that they have *told* them about what is happening (or going to happen). Leaders may genuinely believe that the matter in question has been respectfully discussed and that everyone has had the opportunity to have input. Dialogue, on the other hand, engages others in a process of both reciprocity and respect. What we mean by this is that the participants in the dialogical encounter have a keen sense of inclusion and interpersonal trust. Their thoughts and feelings matter, and they feel safe enough to voice their agreements and disagreements. They have the sense that while they may not impact the final decision or outcome, they at least are able to influence each other toward a deeper understanding of the impending change and the relevance and meaning this holds for them, their team, and their organization. Resonance—a reservoir of positivity that frees the best in people (synchronous vibration)—is established through this process, and team members develop a sense of ownership and motivation.

Our experience shows us that the effectiveness of the change process begins long before the actual introduction of the change itself. Preparation for and clarification of the impending change is central to the successful introduction and implementation of the process. The following model based on the Lewin[25] theory of change shows how preparation becomes a key core aspect of building success.

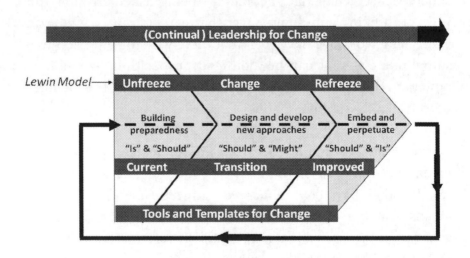

---

[25]   Lewin, K. 'Frontiers in group dynamics'. (1947) In Cartwright, D. (Ed.), *Field Theory in Social Science.*

While we acknowledge that *conformity* is valued by most organizations, we also know that this may represent a low level of actual buy-in. So we make a clear distinction between *followership* and *"sheepership."* True followers believe in and internalize the vision and values of the team and the organization. They embrace the leader's vision and voice their apprehensions and uncertainties appropriately. Those who act like sheep may appear to follow but do so begrudgingly and, over time, sap the energy out of the team and undermine the change process in a passive-aggressive manner. Subtle subversion damages the system and constrains human vigor, resulting in a strong sense of disengagement from the work itself as well as from those who support the change process.

This is not meant to simply denigrate those who act like sheep but rather to suggest the need for a critical evaluation of work environments that lack inclusion, trust, and true leadership. These environments tend to be characterized by a philosophy of individualism and internal competitiveness. "Making it on your own" (it's simply up to you) would appear to be the often unspoken mantra of these organizations. Change is typically a forced procedure lacking in any form of sophistication or understanding of how to truly engage people in the real process of change. "Why don't they simply buy into it?" is representative of what we refer to as *the tyranny of reason.* However, being *reasonable* must include a holistic understanding of both the desired change (task) and the impact and meaning that this holds for those affected by the change (relationship). Without this, the cost in human terms is predictably high, as is the cost in productivity, quality, and sustainable, long-term organizational success.

While the concept of change is usually spoken of in generic terms, we must acknowledge that the range may be from small to massive. Either way, we realize that even apparently minor changes (the moving of one's office or desk from here to there) can create great discomfort for the recipient of that change. Likewise, major change (restructuring of the business) can also elicit strong emotion from those affected. There is no accounting for the individualistic and subjective responses to change—we make it up ourselves! However, conscious leaders will be cognizant of the uniqueness of individual reactions and develop a differential approach to accommodate others as much as possible. The power of empathy plays an important role in facilitating a change process. But it is also important to understand that breakdown is often the source of breakthrough. Besides, we must weather the storm.

Finally, change happens in the *in between*—from concept to collaboration to implementation. With regards to our task and relationship perspective, any change process should hopefully enhance both the organization and all those who are impacted by it: employees, customers, shareholders, and the larger community. Building buy-in and momentum gives power to the change process. Momentum has a life energy of its own, creating power to include all, even the skeptics (and we're all skeptical), and to overcome obstacles and setbacks. The altering of fixed views and set paradigms needs to be approached with the wisdom of understanding and not with the crudeness of the sledgehammer. When change is constructed as an empowering process, based on consideration, respect, and emotional intelligence, then all participants and recipients will experience a sense of dignity and personal worth and move forward with optimism.

Barriers to Effective Communication

Before we move ahead, let's briefly talk about barriers to effective communication and look at two exercises we use. First, the barrier born of an unwillingness to address confrontation, which is always an aspect of change—personal or collective. Based on the work of Lefton and Buzzotta (2004), our research into the question of conflict resolution (Smyth, 2006) is presented in the chart. This reflects a matrix around addressing disagreement, with the percentage of the population that typically falls into each category.

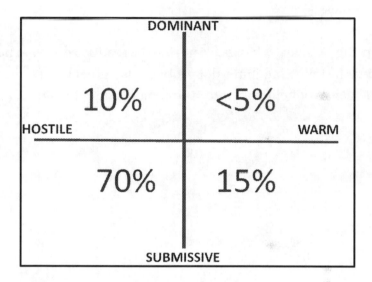

The majority of people (70 percent) will be inclined to shy away from dealing with interpersonal issues, tending to be submissive ("They are doing it *to* me") and hostile ("Because I am not willing to engage, I will be resistant"). This form of passive-aggressive behavior depletes energy and adds to poor workplace morale. The opposite of this is that less than 5 percent of the working population typically deals with issues in a dominant ("I'm prepared to raise the issue because it needs to be dealt with") and warm ("This is not about attacking anyone, and I want to work with you to resolve it") manner. This represents the attitude of "power with" others. The graphic also shows dominant-hostile behavior (10 percent) as being overt, reactive, and controlling ("power over" others). It seems that about 15 percent of the population will be submissive but warm. Essentially, when faced with the prospect of interpersonal conflict, most of the time we don't know where we stand with each other. Our aim is to contribute to the establishment of environments that mostly approximate the "dominant-warm" quadrant of behavior. This is the quadrant of behavior for the development of trust, empowerment, and effectiveness.

Second, to be able to change we need to be ready to drop old habits. We find the following "nine-dot problem" is a great way to illustrate the challenge of being open to "thinking outside the box."

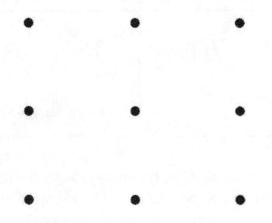

So how would you connect all the dots? The rule is that you must keep your pencil on the paper, and you can only draw four straight lines to connect them all. (The answer is at the back of the book.)

CHAPTER 7

EFFECTIVE INTEGRATION OF TASK

AND RELATIONSHIP

Spending time on building effective relationships is often seen by those involved as a "feel good" exercise. However, it is also true that many efforts to build effectiveness through enhanced task approaches also fail; examples would be money spent on training programs, new business systems, and process re-engineering. What is required is integration, and this becomes an issue of organizational culture. Civilizations take centuries to develop a cultural uniqueness, and in the Western world, there is a desire for speed and making things happen quickly. The issue often becomes a lack of compatibility between building and sustaining an effective culture and managing change. We believe that organizations are a bit like jigsaw puzzles because they are composed of many pieces that must fit together; rather like the constant jostling between plates on the earth's crust, there will always be pressure between competing aspects of an organization's approaches, but as long as there is a sharing of common goals (mission) and common behavior (values), then the effect of change can be made within this context.

Often cultures are damaged or destroyed by change; we developed a simple way of showing this years ago based on how the core of the traditional Plan, Do, Check, Act (PDCA) (or sometimes referred to as Plan, Do, Study, Act) model for management was impacted when organizational change occurs:

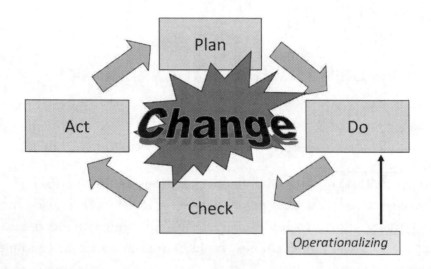

Organizations operate through planning, doing, checking, and adjusting (or acting) based on what they see; organizational change affects how every piece of this model fits together. In addition, organizational effectiveness is the *combination* of how well an organization actually conducts each segment of this model. Over the years, we have asked organizations how well they carry out each element of this model; it has been instructive to see the results over that time. The questions asked are as follows:

- (P) Plan: How well does your organization plan (i.e., understand the reality of where they are today; have a clear understanding of the vision, mission, goals, and objectives as well as expected values and behavior)?

- (D) Do: How well does your organization convert the intent outlined in your high-level plans and expected outcomes into the reality of planning and executing the day-to-day work?
- (C) Check: How effective is your performance-management system (your approaches to measurement and feedback) in monitoring both the outcomes of your plans against actual results as well as the day-to-day management of those projects, initiatives, processes, activities, and tasks through which these outcomes are actually generated?
- (A) Act: How well does your organization take a proactive approach based on the facts from your measurement system to making organizational change versus a reactive approach that seems to say, "Don't confuse me with the facts, just do this"?

When people think through this approach, it is often startling to see both the actual scores and the ranges that exist and underlie the whole issue of organizational effectiveness. One key challenge here is that senior managers (versus the folks in the trenches) sometimes see this issue of integration through a set of rose-colored glasses.

Aspect of Management	Typical Range	Cumulative
Planning (Intent – what you want to do)	60% - 70%	60% - 70%
Doing (Executing the work)	50% - 90%	30% - 63%
Checking (Monitoring and measuring)	50% - 70%	15% - 44%
Acting (Using the results to change if needed)	50% - 70%	8% - 31%

What the results appear to say is that if organizations are honest about their effectiveness, then the best we can expect from their management system is a 31 percent rate of effectiveness (and this could be as low as 8 percent). The great news here is what a wonderful opportunity for improvement exists!

This reflection on an organization as a system aligns with the work of Eliyahu Goldratt and the theory of constraints;[26] Eli makes some very strong claims about how much better organizations could perform if they only looked at their enterprise as a system and optimized all of the pieces so that everything flowed at an optimum level. Eli suggests that organizations could, "over the space of five years, generate a bottom line profit equal to today's revenues." Our conclusion is that we are not alone in thinking there must be something holding this opportunity back.

Years of research have gone into developing management models for effectiveness that have become the basis for awards of excellence in many countries. In the United States, this model is called the Baldrige criteria; in Canada, it is the criteria of the Canadian Awards for Excellence; in Australia, it's the Australian Business Excellence Framework; in the European Union, it's the European Foundation for Quality Management. (And yes, many of these frameworks did in fact come from the initial efforts of attempting to take a holistic approach to quality management, because so many quality initiatives fell short of their desired goals; in many cases, the work on the task side failed to deliver the results because the relationship side was not addressed adequately.)

Some years ago, we researched many of these models and came to the conclusion that they all shared most core components, and

---

[26] Eliyahu M. Goldratt is the author of many books such as *The Goal*, which deals with an organizational system and seeking optimization.

so we created an integrated model and added to it a piece that we believed was missing:

While most models for excellence have results in their framework, including feedback, we felt strongly that in order to build a feedback loop and create a basis for the learning organization, there needed to be an additional segment that dealt with using the feedback to enhance and improve—this ties with the PDCA model.

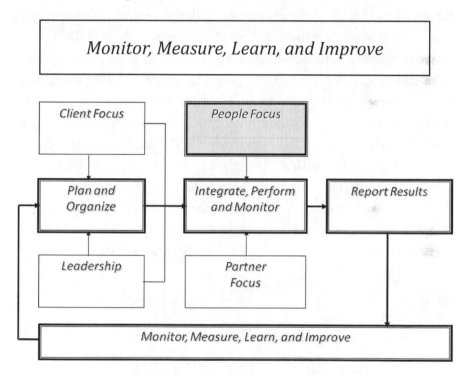

Every model that we reviewed addressed seven core aspects in some way: client focus, planning, leadership, people, process, suppliers, and reporting (outcomes). We believed a key implicit aspect was the ability to be a learning organization, so we added a feedback loop between the results back to planning input. As we developed this model, two things began to become clear. First, it could be closely aligned with the original Deming Plan, Do,

Check, and Act approach, and second, one could look at each of the original seven elements plus the continual-improvement loop and build into these areas key approaches that would link back to aspects of task and relationship management. Thus the model itself, which was developed, adapted, and adopted in varying formats, would provide a great basis for alignment and integration and eventually lead to organizational effectiveness.

Based on this learning, we created an updated, generic management model that focuses on the core aspects an organization addresses in order to operate. Our belief is that once these foundational aspects of organizational activity are in place, they can then be used as a basis for performance management and measurement (e.g., from the highest levels of governance to key organizational activity). This model clearly addresses the importance of the leadership aspect (as part of planning) and then the people aspect (as part of "doing" or work execution). Hence, effective leadership creates the culture and context for organizational activity and success in both what we do (vision and mission) and how we do it (values that drive behavior). Here is a more up-to-date depiction of the model:

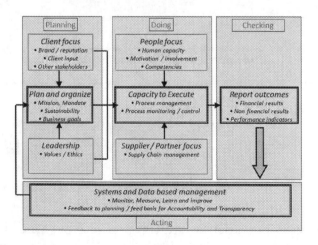

The Task-Relationship Model (TRM) now fits into the framework for excellence; in particular, leadership and the human focus set the direction for behavior, while all other areas focus on tools and methods for enhanced task effectiveness, *but they must be integrated to deliver organizational effectiveness.*

As we showed earlier, organizational direction is initially set through the planning framework, and this is where we will start applying the integration of TRM.

Planning for Effectiveness

This work must involve those responsible for oversight—typically the board and senior management. Boards must set the stage of expectations for both the task and the relationship dimension. If *direction* and expectations of outcomes are clear, then implementation (doing, checking, acting, and improving) have a higher probability of achieving effectiveness. Planning is the foundation of organizational activity, and if this is only 70 percent effective, then it is impossible for any of the following activities to achieve greater than 70 percent levels of performance. The model that we use to focus on setting a clear direction is shown in the chart.

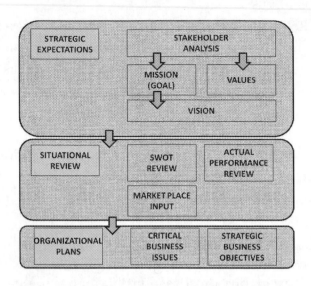

In reality, much of this work is delegated to management, with the board conducting a review as part of the assessment of the business plans; however, the key components must be in place. This three-step approach ensures that a clear direction is set and translated into an effective set of business objectives:

1. **Set strategic expectations.** Who are we and what do we do? This step ensures a clear recognition of who the stakeholders are and the development of a business mission and vision, together with a set of values that reflects expectations of the community. These values are foundational in being able to build effective relationships that support task.

2. **Carry out a reality check and gap analysis**. If the vision is where we *want* to be, then we must know where we are now and where the gaps are.

3. **Decide which gaps are critical to move toward the mission and vision.** Knowing where the gaps are, which ones are critical to sustaining, protecting, and growing the organization?

None of this is new, but this approach integrates task and relationship right from the planning stage. In the twenty-first-century economy, where an organization's competitive advantage comes increasingly from its intangible assets rather than machines and equipment, this alignment with stakeholder interests becomes increasingly valuable. While shareholders are obviously a key stakeholder, an organization's license to operate needs to be increasingly aligned with the expectations of its broader stakeholder community. The four levels of the Toyota approach to management set the culture of the organization as a foundation stone established by the board and shareholders, and thus everything else is built upon this.

While it is beyond this book to explore every one of these steps in detail, a few key points need to be made. First, a Strengths, Weaknesses, Opportunities, and Threats (SWOT) analysis has proven to be very important with clients, because it forms a reality check against both our task performance as well as relationships; what is required for effective planning is 100 percent honesty about today's reality. Many authors and consultants stress the need for an organizational vision, but too often there is a wide gap between the realities of what is happening in the trenches and management's statement of organizational vision, upon which business goals and objectives are set.

We can say then that:

Vision without reality is hallucination and again:
Dishonesty to an organization is like cancer—if not caught
and corrected early enough, it can destroy the whole body.

Another factor that gets in the way of a reality check is the overriding focus on senior management looking good—after all, no one wants to admit to problems! When the confidence of senior management moves into arrogance and an unwillingness to recognize and deal with issues, the seeds of relationship problems are being sown. Peter's many years of study and research into the question of narcissism have revealed many of these problems and illustrates the damaging effect that a narcissistic leader can have on an organization (as well as personal relationships).

You cannot build effective relationships within an organization if staff feels that the direction set by management is out of touch with reality. Determining an organization's strengths, weaknesses, opportunities, and threats is a key starting point in developing an effective business plan.

Observation example

In late 2009 and 2010, Toyota, once revered for its product quality and commitment to client focus, suffered some devastating quality problems. It had been rumored that the one thing that Toyota was most afraid of when it reached #1 in the global automotive rankings was just that—being #1. This can often lead to a feeling of superiority that sometimes results in an unwillingness to accept that there are problems. It also knew that its business was growing ever more complex to manage.

In an article published by Wharton Business School called "Under the Hood of Toyota's Recall: A Tremendous Expansion of Complexity," John Paul MacDuffie lays out the results of an interview with Takahiro Fujimoto, an economics professor at the University of Tokyo and a leading authority on Toyota's production system. The following is an extract from the conversation:

Fujimoto: "Right. I think this can happen to any company which is confident of its quality. This has happened to other companies in the past, too. When you're very confident of your quality, this is a source of arrogance.

"Back in the 1990s, I saw some of my friends complaining about how Toyota treated people when there was a problem. You know, they go to the dealers and then the dealer reports to Toyota about these problems. But [the customers] tended to get a reaction from the company that said, 'The product must be good. We are confident of the quality of the products. So logically it must be your driving problems.' That made many people very angry. I noticed these kinds of things were happening at first sporadically, but then more frequently. I was always warning that arrogance is the number one enemy of the Toyota philosophy. But they didn't take this seriously until big problems happened. And it was really sad to see that."

Another issue is problems with setting priorities; this has two aspects. First, in many organizations, financial performance tends to trump all other considerations. The financial community struggles with this, as most business plans tend to be thought of as financial plans; however, financial results are outcomes and must be balanced and weighed with the other dimensions of stakeholder relationship building. We are seeing this increasingly in practice, where organizations are starting to resist across-the-board downsizing in recognition of the negative impact that this has, not just on talent retention but also on the ability to maintain relationships with staff. Therefore, we need planning to address critical issues around the core components of organizational effectiveness (e.g., the models we have established). In addition, business planning must take into account expectations, existing performance, critical issues, and business objectives in *both* task and relationship.

We use a multidimensional approach to developing critical business issues from an organizational SWOT, using a template such as the one shown below:

People		
Develop and sustain a positive HR environment	Well-trained work force—100% with training plans	Percentage training plans completed
Talent retention	Minimize loss of critical positions <5% p.a.	Loss of core skills % p.a.
Safe and healthy workplace	Best Practice Safety Levels, with zero LTA and full audit compliance	0 lost time accidents 100% OSHA compliance

Environmental/ Social		
Environmentally responsible	Achieve ISO 14001 certification and compliance at all locations	# of plants with ISO 14001 # of audit NCRs
Client/Satisfied Customers		
Sustained satisfaction	Meet commitments to clients	100% service levels achieved Zero quality defects
	Minimize churn <5% p.a.	Customer loss rate # and %
Responsible Stewardship		
Sustainable profitability	Cost containment	Process cost reduction >5% p.a.
Positive cash flow generation		

Other categories might include partnerships with others, such as distributors and shareholder (e.g., joint venture) partners as well as effective leadership, supply chain management issues, and others, such as community. Readers might begin to see an evolving alignment between this type of organizational management approach and the evolution of corporate social responsibility, and we agree there is a connection.

Human Dimensions, Leadership, and "People"

We have already discussed the importance of leadership in aligning relationships with business reality in chapters 5 and 6. Notice from the overall effectiveness model that we also include in the leadership box "values and ethics," so not only do relationships depend upon the organizational value statements, they also include commitments to be an ethical organization. This fully aligns with research that shows that the tone at the top is a key driver from a risk-management perspective of an organization's potential to act in an ethical manner. The Committee of Sponsoring Organizations'[27] framework recommended to be used by the Public Company Accounting Oversight Board[28] as part of risk assessment under Sarbanes-Oxley (SOX) section 404 reporting is a key reinforcement of this reliance on leadership.

Leadership's key role in developing a basis for an effective relationship is to act consistently in both their personal leadership and management activities (e.g., communications, working with others, approaches to customers and clients, and all other key stakeholders, as well as in the direction they set for the organization). As we discussed in the discussion of governance and the board's responsibility, the CEO is the key link between the expectations as established by the board and the deployment of direction in order to deliver on those commitments. Disagreement or inconsistency between the board and the operational leadership spells disaster, not only for creating an effective workplace but also for effective governance and risk management as a whole. A key aspect of this is the development of organizational policy setting; leadership must ensure that policies are consistent with the commitment to behavioral values. A useful tool for ensuring this is the creation of a validation matrix that lists the values and then scores the policy consistency with each value; failure to reach a minimum level of alignment should result in rethinking policies.

A key area that impacts sustainability of organizational values is when change takes place in the organization, such as new

---

[27]   Originally the Treadway Commission; now see www.coso.org.
[28]   See www.pcaobus.org.

managers, new systems, new customers, or new suppliers, and again leadership plays a key role here. The largest of these is in the area of mergers and acquisitions (M&As); every organization has a unique set of values that defines its culture, and when two organizations are brought together, a major stress factor develops when ensuring that a new consensus is built around a shared set of values.

- In an analysis of over 200 European mergers and acquisitions between 2004 and 2007, business leaders indicated that just 9 percent were "completely successful," and this dropped to 3 percent in the UK (Hay Group).
- In India, about 70 percent of M&A deals fail (McKinsey).
- The range of failure is between 50 and 80 percent (Holthausen, Wharton).
- "My firm has analyzed hundreds of M&A deals over the past two decades, and we've found that shareholders would have been better off in 70 percent of the cases if they'd never set off on the path toward M&A" (Shaun Rein, China Market Research).

We were exposed to an interesting example of this when a potential client was discussing the integration between two quite different well-known consumer companies; they indicated that there were many problems, including the clash of cultures between the acquiring company (which was large and well established) and the other firm, a smaller organization that was agile and faster moving and, to some degree, had built its success on those attributes. So we suggested looking at developing a set of shared values between the two organizations as the basis for rebuilding an effective base for relationships and, through that, gaining success in the opportunities that existed for mutual task achievement. "Oh!" they said, "that's already decided—they are going to be told that our values remain and that these will be what they will be expected to fit into."

Now, we could not argue that the end result may have been that the people from the acquired organization finally accepted the values of the acquiring company as a basis for relationship building, but the sheer fact that they were to have *no* say in any discussion or debate was a major problem. Needless to say, we decided not to pursue the opportunity, as this approach would have guaranteed less then optimum results.

We often hear that people resist change, which we think is incorrect; we believe that people resist being told to change; a key success factor in any change-management initiative is engagement and involvement. Many senior business leaders say there is so much to do on the task side that they don't have time to coddle the employees and spend time in group discussions and meetings to help them feel better. Unfortunately, this is a twentieth-century-based belief system that will not help build a twenty-first-century organization.

> Oliver Wyman, a leading executive-development and change-man-agement consulting practice, was quoted in the June 2010 issue of the magazine *Insurance Day* saying that *"most merger and acquisition (M&A) failures stem from cultural issues such as unreconciled differences among executives; little or no attempt in forging a common vision; disparate ideas about fundamental ways of operating, decision making, and customer management philosophy."*

Oliver Wyman focuses executive attention on these areas; a number of key white papers and documents lay out the criticality of cultural issues relative to effective mergers and acquisitions. The British Chartered Management Institute publishes a

"Checklist" (number 232) for managers relative to "Understanding Organizational Culture," and it makes two great points:

Managers should avoid:

- Assuming that an organization's culture can be fully understood through superficial observation
- Believing that the values expressed, for example, in mission statements, necessarily reflect the values actually practiced by the organization

This focus on culture really does bring us into the people dimension of the models for excellence; it is people who make things happen in the organization. Relating back to our earlier discussion on intangible value, we see that it is the people who:

- Build relationships with clients and customers (that are either adding value or not)
- Build supply chain relationships
- Develop effective processes to minimize the cost and maximize the effectiveness of how work is being done
- Contribute innovation and creativity to the development not only of processes but of products and services
- Build internal relationships so that information and knowledge can be shared effectively between differing areas
- Build external relationships with third parties that aid or block organizational strategy

The traditional belief that people are a cost that needs to be minimized should probably be questioned based on the above; human potential is the greatest wasted asset (not only in organizations but in society as a whole). This value of people rests at the heart of building and sustaining intellectual capital, which is an intangible asset, but *only* if application of the knowledge to task is assured, and that's where organizations often fall down. We developed the following graphic some years ago to illustrate this challenge:

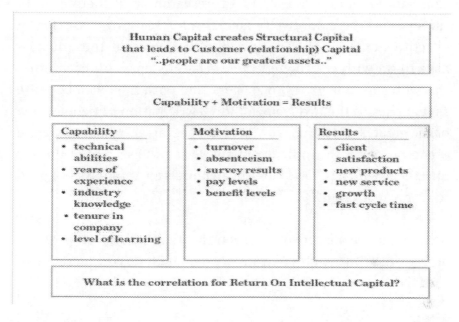

Many organizations talk about people as their greatest assets (which is itself a bit demeaning, as these assets don't belong to the organization and cannot be owned). In addition, we also see from some of the work in the sphere of intellectual capital measurement that organizations should assess their human capital by measures such as counting the years of service or the patents registered; the problem is that this is like measuring my ability to drive based on the number of cars that I own. Talent is only of value if the people who own it decide to apply it (unless you subscribe to the concept of motivation through fear, in which case you may believe that your folks are motivated, but really, who are you kidding?). This graphic illustrates that capability + motivation = results, and the motivation comes from working in an environment where a person is recognized and appreciated—one where relationships are valued.

In their book *First, Break All the Rules*,[29] Buckingham and Coffman identify from years of research and thousands of surveys that there are twelve factors that create the basis for an effective human-resources environment; most of these factors have to do with creating effective relationships with each other and with supervisors and managers, and with the overall culture as it applies to the involvement and participation of people. One of the greatest dilemmas for those managing and leading service organizations is the difficulty of answering the second of the key questions, which is "Do I have the materials and equipment I need to do my work right?"

So an effective alignment between the Task-Relationship Model and an organizational HR strategy would include consideration of the following aspects:

- That ensuring early in the process that the right people are "getting on the bus"—that hiring aligns with organizational values.
- That once "on the bus," the first order of business is a comprehensive orientation that includes clear expectations of both the task and behavior dimensions of the job (we traditionally focus almost entirely on task, often employing on-the-job training).
- That all promotions into leadership only occur with those whose leadership skills equal or exceed their ability

---

[29] Marcus Buckingham and Curt Coffman. *First, Break All the Rules*. New York: Simon & Schuster. 1999.

to manage tasks ("people need leadership, things need managing").

- That all evaluations of performance are aligned with and include both behavioral as well as task achievement (see the next chapter on measurement).
- That investments are continually made in activities that build effective relationships: work assignments between departments, projects, and so on.

The climate within the organization is the crucible within which the human talent rests, and leadership must ensure that this crucible is providing the base upon which the knowledge can be applied willingly and rapidly; key to success in the agile or lean organization is not only zero waste but also the speed of response.

Relationships, Clients, and Customers

Many organizations include in their mission, vision, or values some statements related to their commitment to being customer focused, and this is excellent, but the fact is that few companies actually convert this into practice. How often have we heard that "I hate to do this but I have to follow procedure"? If someone believes that a certain response to a client situation is wrong, then maybe indeed it *is* wrong! In a desire for consistency, organizations have dehumanized the most important relationship to make sure people follow the rules; the problem is—as we discuss later in the process segment—that we cannot write rules for situations we cannot predict. Dealing with clients is often a very unpredictable activity.

In the merger and acquisition business, an increasing proportion of the value of a business is attributed to intangibles—things that we know are important and help the business perform yet for which a financial value cannot be developed (until someone comes along and offers to pay a large sum of money for what they perceive is the value). An effective organization creates value through building relationships with its clients and customers, and these relationships are built by people, on both sides of the transaction. While you may believe your clients do business with your organization because of the organization, in many cases the true linkage (and the "ties that bind") is the relationship between the person who buys and your representative. (It's been said that an effective salesperson actually works 50 percent for your organization and 50 percent for the client!)

An effective, competitive organization is able to build and sustain relationships; this results in lower client turnover, faster resolution of issues, and repeat business. In order to achieve this competitive advantage, all aspects of an organization must be able to work together. In the same way that it takes a village to raise a child, it takes an organization to attract and retain a customer. People within the organization *must* be able to work effectively together, concentrating on shared mission and behavior rather than following independent agendas; only through this can success be achieved.

Has your organization installed a Customer Relationship Management (CRM) system? While this approach to collecting, codifying, and sharing client information is important, it does not build client relationships. People do that—giving them tools to help with the task is good, but allowing them to practice customer-focused behavior is equally as important. A CRM system is a great example of a knowledge-economy approach that focuses on codifying organizational knowledge, but it fails if not supported by a values system that can apply this knowledge. Earlier, we discussed values and their importance as a basis for sharing, upon which effective relationships can be built. Below is an example of how the "Is/Is Not" discussion relative to client-based values might help with translating the statement into behavior.

We seek to create and sustain external relationships that add value for our clients and ourselves	
Is (this means in practice)	*Is Not*
❑ Working on the basis of "we" ❑ Seeking true win/win solutions ❑ Endeavoring to accommodate needs/wants of both parties ❑ Taking the time to understand needs/wants from the relationship ❑ Seeking to build upon and improve the status quo (continuous improvement) ❑ Relationship driven, not event driven ❑ Solving problems from a mutually beneficial approach	❑ Us versus them ❑ Always thinking that we must win (win/lose) ❑ Solving problems at the expense of the relationship ❑ One-dimensional (our way) ❑ Universal/arbitrary ❑ Not thinking application of "procedure" ❑ Reactionary or knee-jerk responses ❑ Planning without client input

This illustrates both the importance of the "Is/Is Not" approach and also the importance of seeking to translate values into the practical aspects of individual roles and positions within the organization.

Nowhere is this more important than the development of service workers in the public or not-for-profit sector. There is no profit to be made from positive behavior toward people who have to deal with you. However, there are tangible benefits through reducing complaints and problem resolution as well as significantly enhanced reputational approaches. This links directly with two gurus of the improvement field: first, the work of Jan Carlzon, who headed SAS from 1991 to 1994 and who coined the phrase "moments of truth"—when an employee and any nonemployee (such as customers) interact. Carlzon stressed that every single one of these moments created (or destroyed) value in the organization's relationship and reputation. Second, Stephen Covey, who coined the phrase the "emotional bank account" to depict the importance of building relationships between people; in good times, we make deposits so that when bad times come, we can make withdrawals without becoming "overdrawn."

Two examples: some years ago, we were involved with implementing the ISO 9001 Quality Management System with the facilities management department of a major Canadian school board (facilities management includes the people who clean the schools and maintain the buildings). A key focus of our work was in focusing on the development of standardized tasks for janitors to complete, and initially there was a desire to proceduralize everything; after all, a janitor's job description usually focuses on the tasks that have to be accomplished versus their role in relationship building. What became quickly apparent was that a janitor's job was as much about relationships as about tasks; these folks had an extremely high level of interaction with *all* types of people—parents, teachers, principals, suppliers, school boards, and of course students. A school principal assessing a high-performing janitor looked way beyond his or her task ability (this was almost a given and defined the effective janitor as one who was successful in responding to others, building relationships, and being flexible in his or her work based on the results). Effective janitors were actually seen as an important contributor to, and a key member of, the school's staff. Conversely, in a few situations, principals (in their role as egocentric leaders) felt they could look down on janitors as lower-class people they could "control and direct" to do their bidding, and invariably the impact of this behavior permeated the whole organization and resulted in an overall lower-performing organization.

The second example deals with developing effective call centers; these have become a core component of many organizations in solving client problems. However, while they provide a key service to sustain relationships, they are costly and often form a significant portion of an organization's budget. So the question organizations face is how to solve this challenge of providing this support in a cost-effective manner. The task approach is often focused on developing clearly scripted responses to client's problems based on an analysis of past conversations; this is then linked to service standards that focus on getting clients off the phone as soon as possible. However, in the process/task-focused zeal to enhance productivity, what is often lost is any sense of empathy with the customer, including listening skills; in addition, even if the listening does take place, this is often not connected to feedback to the rest of the organization and process changes that could alleviate the root causes of the problem. (In addition, some organizations have outsourced their call centers to reduce the cost, only to see satisfaction plummet.)

The balanced organization sees the call center as a window into the world of its customers; if something is a problem for a customer, then it's often because our own processes failed; our instructions for the product were not clear; our salespeople made unrealistic delivery promises; our service process was not working the way it should. This is core business intelligence that is needed to actually improve what the organization does. The success of a call center should be based on the increase in satisfied customers and a decrease in calls being received. If the staff of the call center is seen as a core aspect of the business and listened to in terms of what input the clients are providing, then the level of customer intelligence and focus will improve.

Below we show the results of some research into effective service delivery in the public sector carried out by the Institute of Citizen-Centered Service (ICCS) in Toronto; this research indicated that there were five key drivers for client satisfaction in the provision of public sector services to citizens.

Timeliness: the single most important driver of satisfaction	Need processes designed around client needs plus staff willing to focus on clients needs; example would be willingness of staff to help one another when workloads change.
Staff: customers appreciate knowledgeable staff who "go the extra mile" and make that extra effort	Ability of staff to build relationships that the client sees as positive (process designed to accomplish task needs to be responsive to service providers' needs).
Positive outcome: "I got what I needed"	Relationship: often clients don't get what they "want" but can still end up being satisfied; example would be the ability of a regulatory service: speeding ticket—"I know I was wrong but what mattered to me was the way I was treated."
Ease of access	Process/task heavy: needs to be designed around client needs; knowing the client becomes key to providing an effective response.
Citizens' most recent experience with public services	Heavily relationship based: "Did I come away with a positive experience?" This comes from relationship.

People and the Process Dimension

Organizations spend amazing amounts of money on initiatives to enhance task; particular examples are machinery and equipment, information-technology solutions, and business process-management initiatives, yet so often we hear of failures to achieve the desired outcomes from these investments. Process effectiveness has become a critical success factor for organizational success and in many cases is itself the organization's competitive advantage. Processes typically require people to work together to accomplish a given task, and as such, building effective relationships internally becomes a key challenge. This is where we often hear the "flavor of the month" approach, where management develops a program that is to be implemented in the current fiscal year and pushes ahead, often focusing on the "controlling and directing" aspects of management skills rather than employing areas such as involvement, participation, and listening.

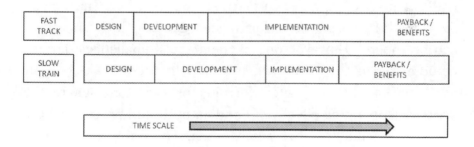

In implementing new initiatives, it takes more time to involve people; design and development are usually rushed through so that implementation can start. That is the "fast track" approach; however, often taking the slow train takes more time for involving people in design and development, but implementation will be much faster, with a resulting overall improvement in getting to the benefits from the change. In addition, the satisfaction with the changes will often be greater, not necessarily because people got their way but because they had a chance to voice their opinion, and in a climate of positive relationships, they will be more apt to take a collaborative view, aiming at consensus building rather than "win/lose." (Fast is slow, slow is fast.)

One of the challenges of understanding task effectiveness under any conditions is that many organizations do not actually manage their core processes; performance measures are often absent, and in many cases, criteria for an effectively functioning process may never have been established. This challenge is prevalent in many service organizations, both for-profit and not-for-profit, such as public sector firms.

Very large organizations, for example banks whose transactional volumes run into millions if not billions, have adopted many manufacturing concepts into their approach to process design and have applied approaches such as Business Process Reengineering (BPR) and Six Sigma; well-defined specifications have been developed for process performance against which measures can be applied. However, one of the greatest challenges that we come across is the "unknown productivity factor," which deals with the gap between a conforming process (one where the process is operating effectively) and an optimum process, where the process could be that much better. The only way to really optimize organizational processes is to listen and respond to the concerns of the people actually working within the process; the challenge here is that processes are typically interdepartmental or interorganizational.

As an example, effective order taking starts with the customer's organization and includes several internal departments; procurement or purchasing involves supplier organizations and again spans several departments. We can broaden this out to design, where many departments are impacted; customer service and many more. The point here is that these processes can *only* be optimized if "silo" management, including "looking for who to blame," is eradicated and replaced by collaboration. This means throwing our lot in with others, both inside and outside the organization, trusting people who we don't always work with and may not know that well, thinking interdependently versus independently. All of these attributes require an organization to have effective working relationships in place. Thus, effective process management is founded on effective interpersonal skills, which rely upon effective relationship building.

A word of warning is probably needed here. Some organizations invest money in employee-profiling approaches, such as Myers-Briggs, which identify individuals into behavioral groups. These are good tools and provide great value; however, building relationships with others requires that we truly understand ourselves, and our opinion is that organizations need to move to a deeper process of human understanding that goes beyond "grouping" and truly focuses on the unique character of each individual. The approach that we use in psychometric assessment tools is discussed in more depth later.

Process management remains a key issue relative to the need for effective relationships; there is a school of thought that believes that codification of processes (e.g., documentation) will enable organizations to capture the knowledge in people's heads and so retain ownership and control of the details that makes the process work and thus become less reliant on people. This was an interesting observation during the 1990s, when many organizations implemented ISO 9001 (the globally recognized quality-management system). Implementation seemed to follow two streams: some focused on a program of defining and documenting every process in the organization and then ensuring that no one deviated from that. Others seemed to recognize that ISO would work as a great framework for quality but that documentation per se was not the nirvana for success that many appeared to believe. These organizations focused on developing documentation more as a framework for training and help when needed, and then empowering people to change, update, and improve processes wherever possible to recognize the reality of learning and improving what we do. Needless to say, those in the latter school tended to build the basis for a learning organization, while the others created a bureaucracy where change and improvement became a chore.

We believe that in the knowledge economy, an excessive focus on documentation is unrealistic; Jan Carlzon, who we mentioned earlier, captured the importance of people within the people/ process framework in his book *Moments of Truth*; Jan was the CEO of SAS from 1981 to 1994, a period during which the Western world was heavily focused on improving the quality of service organizations. Carlzon, together with Claus Moller of Time Manager International (who developed service training programs for SAS), recognized that the key was to "delegate responsibility away from management and allow customer-facing staff to make decisions to resolve issues on the spot." This approach illustrates that in many organizations, quality and service come from managing what cannot be predicted and ensuring a positive outcome rather than focusing on what can be controlled. In every organization, things will occasionally go wrong, and in most cases, it is the ability of the organization to fix the problem that creates the desired level of client satisfaction. If an employee does not feel engaged, supported, and responsible for doing this and is unable to obtain support from others in the organization to do what needs to be done to fix the problem, then the result will be a dissatisfied client.

Let's reflect on the balance required between people and process in a service—and knowledge-based economy to remember why process alone will not achieve the desired outcome of organizational excellence.

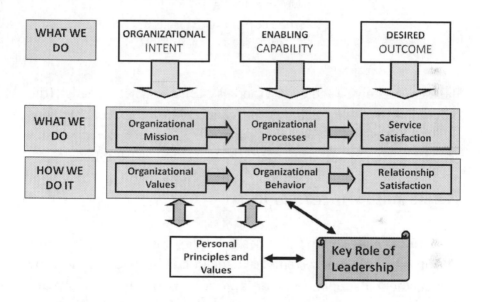

As a final note on process and its dependence on effective relationship management, we can address internal controls; this hooks right back to SOX, where the initial assessment on organizational control risk starts with the climate that leadership creates. This is a strong and powerful competitive issue because, as Nick teaches financial managers, "the key to success is to remain just in control." Excessive controls breed bureaucracy, which defeats innovation and creativity; an absence of controls encourages fraud, unethical conduct, and other aspects of organizational behavior that create significant risk.

IT'S ALL ABOUT ACHIEVING BALANCE

NEED FOR CONTROL
- Effective reporting
- "Just enough"
- Risk management

NEED FOR INNOVATION
- Local leadership
- Operational autonomy
- Flexibility

Maintaining a
small company
mindset

Balance can only be achieved if there is clarity on what is needed (the outcomes) and what behavior is acceptable (the approach). Thus the T-R approach is critical for achieving organizational balance and delegation of authority to those closest to the front lines.

People and Partners/Suppliers

As outlined above, core processes extend outside the organization. Quality-management systems have included effective selection and management of suppliers as a core system component for many years. As we described in chapter 3, today's relationships with external third parties is critical, whether this be suppliers, contractors, outsourcing partners, or joint venture partners. More and more, we are dealing with outsiders to get the job done, and what's more, we no longer own these capabilities. The task of effective buying and selling still rests on the ability to negotiate a good deal; pressure on suppliers to reduce costs will always be important, but today, the way that this is achieved creates either partnerships or dictatorships. In the same way that an unmotivated employee will hold back on his or her willingness to share innovation and creativity, so will suppliers withhold support if they cannot trust their partner.

In his book about being the low cost bidder,[30] Dr. David Anderson discusses how the techniques applied by GM in supplier negotiations sowed the seed for the unwillingness of suppliers to share innovation; in fact, it kept their best resources from working with GM and Chrysler. Even Toyota needs lower prices and believes in the process of continuous improvement to achieve it. Once again, it's not about the task itself but about how the task is achieved.

A willingness to build relationships permeates all of these discussions; another example comes from the world of "shared services." One client is the information technology (IT) group within a multibillion-dollar government department. Initially, this IT group only serviced other internal clients; however, a few years ago, the department was split in two, and one section became a standalone unit that itself took over (amalgamated with) several other departments. The IT group now had both internal and external clients to whom monthly and annual charges had to be made for cost recovery. IT was a strong organization and had traditionally distributed costs based on a process of allocations—estimating what costs should go where. However, the external department now started to ask exactly what they were paying for and demanding that these costs be justified. The IT department knew that to get into this would both require more work but would also give greater insights into where the money was going; thus the initial response was to "stiff arm the client" and focus on a win/lose strategy. At one point, it became possible that the new department, which actually set up its own facilities and mirrored what services were being provided, would increase overall costs. Win/win would have been to recognize that in a world

---

[30]   *"Build-to-Order & Mass Customization; the Ultimate Supply Chain Management and Lean Manufacturing Strategy for Low-Cost On-Demand Production without Forecasts or Inventory,"* by Dr. David M. Anderson, (2008, CIM Press).

of shared services, we have to be open and seek win/win results. What was needed was an attitudinal change on both sides, where a relationship could be built based on trust and openness, seeking the right overall decisions. Here we had two partners that had not invested in building relationships that were now suffering because the task of managing IT costs could not be quickly addressed.

Many technology organizations subcontract post-sales servicing of their equipment to third parties that specialize in that particular aspect of technology. To the client, the person responding to the service call is by definition representing the brand of the product being supported (as a customer, I hold the manufacturer responsible and care little about the arrangements that have been put in place to get the job done). However, if the manufacturer's expectations about how clients are responded to and treated (their values) are not shared by the subcontractor, then pretty soon the lack of client focus on the part of the subcontractor will have a negative impact on the brand value of the manufacturer. Thus specifications in terms of contractual arrangements and performance criteria with the subcontractor must include both task and relationship aspects, and the selection of the partner must be assessed against both these aspects if the relationship is going to succeed.

Internal Controls and Task/Relationship

As we have moved into the twenty-first century and the knowledge economy, we have been surrounded by governance issues: scandals, fraud, excessive risks being taken, misappropriation of shareholder funds. Starting with scandals such as the "Whitewater" affairs in the 1980s and Barings Bank, the siren song became "Directors are asleep at the wheel" and "We need better systems of risk management." These calls led initially led to investigative commissions and globally inquiries (Cadbury Commission, CoCo, etc.) that came up with some renewed approaches to risk management. Then we had the "dot com meltdown," when it became obvious that understanding and effectively governing knowledge-based organizations was not working with the old approaches to corporate governance (Shepherd, 2005). What was needed was something new; however, before this could be achieved, we had the challenges of Tyco and Enron, which resulted in SOX being enacted in the United States to clean up corporate accountability.

The problem in all of this is that a knowledge economy, together with an agile organization structure, depends upon people acting individually (and often independently). This is why it has become increasingly critical today to establish values and embed them in the corporate culture. Some of the work that we have begun development on over recent years has included thinking through how internal controls are developed organizationally. Our goal has been to develop a framework for effective controls that takes into account the increasing dependency on human behavior. The chart below illustrates some of our initial thinking in developing controls that are effective because they are based on buy-in to compliance.

			Low **CONSULTATION LEVEL** High

<table>
<tr>
<td rowspan="2">CONTROL LEVEL
High</td>
<td>IMPOSED CONTROLS
• Theoretical-based control
• Process bias
• Standards based
• Ease of auditability
• Accounting bias
• Operational resistance
• Controls added as a burden</td>
<td>COLLABORATIVE CONTROL
• Outside-in approach
• Enterprise risk based
• Balanced to operational reality
• Operational bias
• Broad-based approach
• Operational "buy in"
• Controls integrated</td>
</tr>
<tr>
<td>PASSIVE / REACTIVE CONTROL
• Inside-out approach
• Lack of understanding reality
• Risks not effectively known</td>
<td>NICE GUY CONTROL
• Meeting other's needs
• Focused on harmony only
• Known risks ignored</td>
</tr>
<tr>
<td>Low</td>
<td colspan="2" align="center">Low   CONSULTATION LEVEL   High</td>
</tr>
</table>

While this remains an emerging area of study, we believe that understanding the effectiveness (or not) of internal controls must include aspects of behavior.

Relationships, Results, and Improvements

One of the final aspects of linking relationships back to organizational models for excellence is the aspect of results: the ability to check and know that what was planned is actually happening. This aspect must be integrative, in that if it is to mirror corporate direction based on mission and behavior, then it must assess both task and relationship performance. What is management all about?

This graphic is based on the well-known Plan, Do, Check, and Act model attributed to Dr. Deming (and earlier to Walter Shewhart) and is widely used in improvement cycles, including a modified version in the popular Six Sigma framework, where it is called the

146

DMAIC (Define, Measure, Analyze, Improve, Control) cycle. In all cases, it can really be referred to as "Management 101." This is what forms the basis of management: starting with planning what you want to do (links back to our governance discussions). How is management going to do it? How will we know what is happening? The whole basis of performance-measurement systems, including the very relevant work some years ago by Kaplan and Norton in *The Balanced Scorecard*, deals with multidimensional measurement to achieve organizational strategy, and finally knowing what's going on from the measurement system having a process to respond to it.

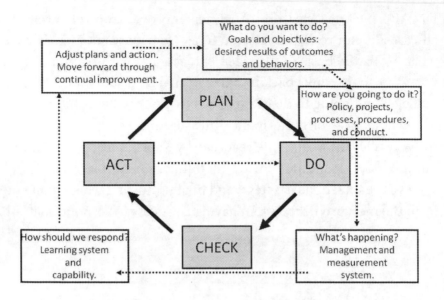

Boards, leaders, and managers who focus on measuring task and don't focus on relationships are missing a key component of their responsibility, and given the criticality of organizational capacity related to its relationships, they may in fact be watching over a declining business. The concentration on financial performance, being a lagging indicator, can be a very dangerous activity if hidden beneath the numbers is the reality that short-term financial gain is being achieved through the strategic depletion of the organization's core capability to perform (i.e., its relationships and through that its reputation).

Enhanced Task through Foundational Relationships—Recap

In this section, we focused on the development of an excellent organization; we used the key components shared by many national excellence frameworks as a basis for focusing on what the main elements of task are. Here are our key learnings:

1. Planning: In order to be effective, today's organization, operating in a world of intangibles and knowledge management, must place equal emphasis on planning, execution, and measurement systems on what needs to be done (mission) and how it is to be done (behavior).

2. Leadership: Leaders set the expectations and create the climate that allows the building of effective relationships (or else allows silos and independence to develop).

3. Customer focus: Customer and client satisfaction results from getting both the outcome that they expect and a positive experience when dealing with the organization.

4. Process: Organizational capacity, and hence sustainability and competitiveness, is based on a combination of tangible capability (tools and equipment) and intangible capability (knowledge, innovation, relationships):

    a. Effective tasks need effective tools supported by effective relationships that build a foundation of communication, collaboration, and cooperation; investments in new tools may not bring the desired results unless supported and used in a collaborative work environment.

5. Suppliers and partners: Today's organizations are highly collaborative, involving both internal and external linkages; to be effective, positive relationships between the people who make up these relationships make them work effectively.

6. Results: Measurement systems must reflect a combination of both task results and behavioral results in order to assess progress to plans.

7. Learning and improvement: The foundation of continual improvement is people's willingness to apply their capacity of innovation and creativity to the work task; this depends

on self-motivation, the foundation of which is based on positive relationships with others.

If an organization wishes to enhance effectiveness, it must invest in both the infrastructure to support the employees in achieving their tasks plus invest in building relationships so that these tasks can be executed effectively in collaboration with others.

CHAPTER 8

KNOWING IT'S REAL: BUILDING AND

USING MEASUREMENTS

While intellectually most people realize that investments in human potential will bring organizational benefits, today's competitive situation often has decision makers looking for "payback" from developmental activity. We believe that our goal is to help improve organizational effectiveness and through this gain competitive advantage through improved productivity as well as an ability to attract and retain talent. As a result, we start out by focusing on the journey to organizational effectiveness as the main goal; while we want to create a workplace that people actually enjoy being part of, the ultimate outcome must be a competitive and sustainable organization.

Using the matrix, we see that survival comes from combining effective management (of task) with effective leadership (of people). While organizations that focus on task can demonstrate delivery of results, the reality is that this approach is often not sustainable. In fact, in a knowledge-based society, we end up with valuable talent fleeing the organization. However, in the same way, excessive focus on relationship building can be just as damaging, as task gets relegated to a secondary position. The paradigm we operate in is that relationships are the effective enablers of task achievement.

Thus, to justify investments in building relationships, we need to be able to answer the question about what the payback is, and the best way to address this is to look at the symptoms of an ineffective organization and try to reverse them.

Kaplan and Norton[31] developed an important step forward in their book on organizational performance measurement, in which they postulated that achievement of strategy was the result

---

[31]   Robert S. Kaplan and David P. Norton. *The Balanced Scorecard.* Boston: Harvard Business Press. 1996.

of managing the business system and not any one component. They focused on four key areas that should be addressed:

- Financial dimension
- Internal business process dimension
- Customer dimension
- Learning and growth dimension

This approach was one of the earlier efforts to identify the need for a broad-based performance-measurement system. Interestingly enough, the concepts mirror the work of the various management models for excellence that we discussed earlier, within which the results dimension required an organization to have the capability of monitoring and measuring the effectiveness of all of its key activities. What we propose is similar and was discussed in Nick's earlier book on corporate governance.[32]

Measuring Leadership Effectiveness

While we can spend much time discussing overall performance measurements, let's focus here on the core aspects of building effective relationships. What are the outcomes that we would expect from an organization that has a productive workforce that is fully engaged in and committed to organizational activity, and how would we find out? This top ten list provides a good starting point:

1. High level of innovation and improvement in task (process improvement/new products, etc.)
2. Positive responses from clients, customers, or citizens (whom we serve)

---

[32] Nick Shepherd. *Governance, Accountability, and Sustainable Development: An Agenda for the 21st Century.* Toronto: Carswell Thomson. 2005.

3. Positive reputation with key stakeholders (e.g., community)
4. Low/acceptable staff turnover
5. Low/acceptable levels of absenteeism
6. Fast resolution of problems and issues (customer complaints, nonconformance, etc.)
7. Level of development of internal staff (e.g., hiring from within and development plans)
8. "Living the values" as evidenced by employee feedback on leadership conduct
9. Positive responses to surveys such as the ACT tool (example in appendix)
10. Readiness for change (new initiatives are rapidly implemented)

In looking through these top ten items, we can immediately see a fit within the scorecard context: process aspects, customer aspects, learning and growth, and, finally, financial aspects. A key link here is the connection between process management and financial aspects. If we accept that a key component of a competitive organization is its ability to minimize costs, then innovative ideas should show up in process measures such as lower cycle times, zero defects, and, most importantly, a lower transaction cost for core business processes as measured on a cost-per-transaction basis. This is an absolute driver of an organization's ability to achieve competitive advantage through the harnessing of employee talent. Only through constant lowering of costs can an organization remain competitive; whether a not-for-profit that is striving to do more with less, such as governments delivering more services without higher tax revenues, or for-profit organizations being able to compete in the global marketplace. It is this ability to link talent to resource consumption that connects relationship building to more effective outcome through task improvement.

In Nick's governance book, a section was devoted to the role of leadership in ensuring that an organization's "intangible value" was being sustained. This is a key outcome of effective engagement, but financial reporting fails to crystallize this unless an organization is sold; in this case, buyer and seller agree on a price, and the difference between the book value (the historical value of the business as recorded in the accounting records) and the amount the buyer is willing to pay is called "goodwill." This is the number that a point in time crystallizes the value of the combined intangibles. Effective organizations today seek to assess what these intangibles are and then strive to develop metrics that assess their ongoing sustainability and growth. It is irresponsible for any leader today—let alone a board of directors—to entrust the sustainability of their enterprise to a management team and then not track and monitor the total value or worth of the enterprise. This is why the top ten metrics identified above must become part of mainstream reporting and accountability.

The following table is provided as additional thoughts on the types of measures that might be adopted, in developing metrics that link back to leadership:

- ☐ # of managers who have completed leadership assessments (psychometrics)
- ☐ # of managers who have received coaching on leadership improvement skills
- ☐ # of managers who have completed leadership training
- ☐ # of managers who are rated 5 as "effective leaders" on 5-point scale survey (with subset data such as communications, problem resolution, etc.)
- ☐ # of managers with completed EQ assessments (emotional quotient is a measure of emotional intelligence)

- [ ] High trust rating—4 on a 5-point scale—between employees and management within the organization
- [ ] Tenure of CEO and other managers
- [ ] Promotions/growth from within
- [ ] Leadership capacity based on 360-degree assessment results (i.e., actual results and alignment)
- [ ] # Grievances/staff problems related to leadership skill-based issues
- [ ] # Suggestions for improvement from employees supported or championed by managers and supervisors
- [ ] Leadership time allocation by managers and supervisors (MBWA, etc.)
- [ ] # Internal recognition and awards involving managers on teams
- [ ] # Hours managers and supervisors spend on group or team interaction development activity
- [ ] Hours managers and supervisors spend per year communicating plans and organizational vision

Ultimately, improvements in relationship building can be measured from both an activity perspective (what is going on) and an outcome perspective (how are we doing in key aspects of outcomes—both from an operational perspective as well as from creating sustainability by maintaining and building our talent base).

CHAPTER 9

TASK AND RELATIONSHIP IN PRACTICE:

CASE STUDIES

In this segment of the book, we will offer suggestions and ideas based on real-life experiences we have had with clients in developing and implementing our approach.

Case 1   Manufacturing Subsidiary of a Family Business

Background to Our Participation

This manufacturing business employed about sixty people when we started and grew to nearly two hundred over the next few years. One of the current executives, who was also a shareholder, had been brought into the family business by her father and was acting in the role of vice president of human resources. In order to expand her business experience, her father appointed her president of this wholly owned manufacturing facility, which provided products for the railroad freight car industry. This subsidiary had traditionally been run by a fairly autocratic, top-down manager whose style was diametrically opposite to that of the newly appointed president, who was therefore faced with the task of trying to change the management culture. It was at this point that she turned to Peter for help with the people development side of the business. Peter worked with the company for a short time, at which point the president indicated her desire to move forward from developing the team itself into development of the team's management skills. It was at this point that Nick became involved and started to work on both implementing a process for planning and linking the results of the planning to clear accountability and responsibility, which would then become the basis for further delegation of responsibility as well as incentives and pay for performance.

Task: Relationship Development

Peter had made great strides in developing the individuals on the management team through developing their awareness of self, facilitated by the use of a well-known psychometric assessment tool.[33] The team was beginning to work well together, and so it was into a fertile field that Nick started to sow the seeds of effective task management through the development of a business planning process.

What became apparent in the fairly early stages was that you only know whether team development is working when you subject the team to the rigors of shared goals. This is not a new finding but one that clearly reinforced our belief that organizational

---

[33]   The current tool we use is from Lumina Learning; see commentary in chapter 10.

development is not an "either/or" model where you can work on the human dimension or the task dimension, but an interactive process through which the team moves forward, then slips back and recovers and moves forward once again. In fact, this is the foundation of any process of continual improvement. (This reality is consistent with the new six-stage team development model that we developed that allowed for the continual correction and moving forward of a group striving to become an effective team.)

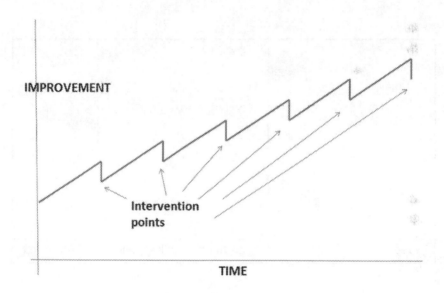

Intervention points: The coaching continuum

In this client's case, the team found strong disagreement starting to develop when agreement and achievement of the organization's goals started to interfere with what they saw individually as their personal goals: "Why should I give up some valuable time that I need to spend on achieving my goals, just so you can achieve yours?" Without intervention to address this, the team would have gradually slipped back into a collection of individuals purporting to be a team but in fact acting as individuals.

This learning is again not new, as the four traditional stages of team development, shown in the chart below, demonstrate. In the second phase of "storming," if nothing is done to effectively facilitate this, there will be no chance of the team successfully achieving the "norming" and the "performing" stages. Typically, teams with no intervention at this stage will fail.

High				
Low				
Expectations	Forming	Storming	Norming	Performing

The four stages of (traditional) team development

This is where, in our Core Model, we address Deliberation as the stage where such potential conflicting issues are addressed and which then forms the basis to move forward to the Amalgamation and Consolidation stages.

This challenge clearly indicated two key issues: first, that improved task effectiveness *depends* upon a solid and sustainable relationship base, and second, team development is not a singular process but an ongoing one. Effective development is about sustained coaching—after all, the coach doesn't go home when the game starts! All the preliminary learning and development needs ongoing support when the approaches are put into practical life situations.

Additional Challenges and Learnings

As we moved forward from the team development and planning stage, it became apparent that because of the top-down management style previously applied, the managers of this organization had been placed in their positions because, from a style perspective, they were good at operational application but not necessarily at strategic thinking. In addition, because the previous general manager had delegated little or no management control, the managers had never been taught to understand and interpret financial and cost information and so found it very difficult, when they were delegated the task of managing, to actually understand what had to be done.

How often is it that this occurs? We promote managers into new roles or we bring in a new leader with a different style, and we wonder why it doesn't work. Part of the coaching therefore became finding out the missing competencies for these managers and helping them learn and apply the new skills required for effective performance on the job. Their jobs hadn't changed, but the way in which they were expected to execute them had, so without this additional support, they would have been subjected to a higher risk of failure. Thus again effectiveness is a combination of both task (tools and skills) and relationships.

Evolution of the Team Development and Ongoing Benefits

The process of developing task and relationship continued for approximately three years, at which time the president moved back to another corporate position. What were the benefits of this intervention?

- Individuals on the team took on greater responsibility and accountability for their leadership role and made the decision to develop and commit to the organizational goals both personally and as a member of the team.
- Each manager developed a greater awareness of the work of other departments and became more sensitive to the importance of collaboration, coordination, and communication, and as they now understood each other better, they could be more open in their communication.
- The president was able to do her job (i.e., leave operational day-to-day management decisions to the individual managers), thus becoming more productive personally.
- Through this change, the president became more externally focused and was able to devote time to business development, which had not been happening in the past.
- Key operational performance indicators (product quality, on-time delivery, cost compliance) improved, and problems were dealt with faster through acceptance and fixing rather than seeking how to shift the blame, thus enhancing client satisfaction.
- Overall, the subsidiary grew its revenues to levels not previously achieved and generated both profits and positive cash flow at a level not seen before, such that it was the highest-performing subsidiary in a group of over thirty companies.

- The president was promoted and the operations manager took over as general manager; while the company suffered in the recent economic downturn, it was able to weather the storm, in a business where client purchasing almost dried up completely, yet maintained a positive cash flow.

This organization is similar to many small- to medium-sized businesses where the management team was managed in a top-down style for many years. Bringing in a new leader with a new style as well as different ideas of management tools is a foundation for making change, but without participation and involvement of the key managers, there will be resistance to change. Resistance to change is a real and practical issue, yet the more people understand themselves and why they respond to situations the way that they do, the more effective they will be in handling change effectively and delivering the results to the organization.

Case 2   Resource Industry: Joint Venture

Background to Our Participation

This organization, based in Alaska, was projected to be one of the five largest gold-producing mines in the world. The mine has moved through a number of ownership situations and is today a joint venture between two US mining companies. Nick was approached after giving a seminar on "Leadership for Financial Managers" in British Columbia and asked about his experience of working with management and leadership teams; in particular, this client had problems in accountability and responsibility of individual managers for collective compliance responsibilities of the organization as a whole. After listening to the problem, Nick felt that the client would benefit from the task-relationship approach;

163

although a task issue appeared to be the challenge, the root cause seemed to be relationships at the management team level.

Task: Relationship Development

In carrying out our research prior to our first team meeting, it quickly became clear that the two joint venture partners had developed from very different cultures; one is a long established mining company with global operations that, because of its size, has well-developed policies and procedures as well as clear career paths for its managers and leaders. The other partner comes from what is often referred to as the "junior mining stocks," and although a successful company in its own right, it attributed much of its success to its lack of corporate bureaucracy and its ability to move fast and be flexible. In addition, this junior mining company had in fact been the subject of a hostile takeover attempt by the larger company that was now its partner! Why was all this important? Because the management team at the joint venture was composed of a mixture of key managers who came from each of the parent companies and brought with them strong allegiances to their particular organization. So we were prepared for some interesting initial discussions.

Our first meeting focused on developing a relationship with the leadership team; nobody on the team had worked with us before, and we needed to assess the climate and then affirm the plan that we intended to implement to help them move forward. Based on this, we conducted a three-day mini retreat where we introduced the Task-Relationship Model and talked about aspects of human behavior and team development; we spent time listening to the team members express their opinions and discuss the challenges faced by the company. We also talked about the concept of organizational behavior from the perspective of both what the leadership team members felt was important and what they felt was important in dealing with key stakeholders.

This latter part developed into a critical discussion, as it quickly became apparent that a key factor of the joint venture's history was the development, over a period of about fourteen years, of a solid working relationship with the local rural population's native corporation, who owned the rights to the gold reserves. The future workforce was to largely come from the local population, and success of the overall venture over the long run, including areas such as permitting and startup timing, would depend upon establishing and sustaining a trusting commitment between the joint venture and key stakeholders such as these. This area was of particular interest to us, as we believe that this working relationship was a key asset of the organization, even though it was not recognized as a specific item anywhere on the financial records. In today's competitive environment, building these types of underlying capabilities and capacities has become the leading factors in creating organizational value.[34]

At the first meeting, a lot of discussion centered on the different corporate cultures that each team member came from and the individual's feeling of what was good and bad about "the other company." It became apparent that there were in fact two teams here—one from each parent company—and that a key barrier

---

[34] For more reading on this topic, read *Unrecognized Intangible Assets: Identification, Management and Reporting*, written by Nick Shepherd and Mary Adams and published by the Institute of Management Accountants (IMA) US.

to develop the basis for effective relationships was a lack of trust between team members and the belief that members of each team did not share any values or beliefs. This was a classic resistance-to-change issue and was reinforced by the fact that each team member had other members who they could commiserate with, and they reinforced each other. We came to the following conclusions that established the steps we would need to take going forward:

1. There would be little improvement in task, especially tasks that required collaboration (which most do at the executive team level), until the relationship issues were addressed.

2. There would be no improvement in relationships until individuals on the team came to an agreement that there were no "good and bad guys" on the team but they were in this together, and success or failure was their choice.

3. There would be no moving away from "good and bad guys" until this team defined a set of organizational values that they wanted to underpin the behavior of *their* business unit (and that this aligned with *both* their parent organizations).

4. There would be no leadership team in *this* business unless every member made a commitment to this joint venture and balanced this with an effective strategic linkage with the parent organizations.

5. It would be difficult to develop a set of organizational values unless team members were open and honest with each other and truly expressed their feeling and beliefs without fear of ridicule and rejection.

This set of findings is similar to that which many organizational leadership teams experience; after all, to achieve leadership, each member needs to have a strong commitment to his or her organization and its values and, in many cases, develop an overriding identity with their organization, seeing others as the competition.

> This is one of the key challenges of mergers and acquisitions (M&As), especially in service organizations, where relationships are more critical, and why many fail. Often called the "clash of cultures," the problems come from an inability to "unfreeze, change, and refreeze"[35] to become a renewed organization and culture. Without professional intervention and facilitation, reactive human behavior takes over and the organization becomes nothing more than a collection of people who work together, with no underlying relationship building, which is the lubricant that converts people's capacity into effective task execution and outcomes.

Steps to Success

The follow-up retreat was preceded by managers taking psychometric assessments, which were conducted on-line. This formed the basis of Peter's first day at the retreat, where he explained the concepts behind the personal assessment results. Managers were then given the option of sharing information among each other, and this formed the beginning of opening up the dialogue between team members. The more each person understood his or her own personality and why he or she responded to situations

---

[35] For more on unfreeze, change, and refreeze, see the work of Lewin as well as other models of effective change management.

in a certain way, the more he or she became self-aware; the more self-awareness that developed, the more willingness there was to recognize that others on the team may, in fact, see things in a different way from a different perspective. However, acceptance of this as being of value to the team was not yet developed, as it tended to reaffirm a problem rather than suggesting a solution.

Another part of this retreat dealt with how the team expected the organization and the people within it to act with each other; this often becomes a fairly emotional discussion, as behavior is important to people, and the values that underpin our behavior are key building blocks in developing effective relationships. One particular part of this discussion that took some time was when the individual who was instrumental in building the relationships with the local communities explained how he had done this and what the founding principles were. He passionately expressed that some of the new policies had the potential to destroy the work that he had achieved over fourteen years, and if that happened, the ability of the organization to move forward smoothly with its key stakeholders would be jeopardized.

This discussion was key to moving forward, as it illustrated to the other team members how important this was both to the individual as well as the organization; it also showed that people develop personal interpretations of the values and belief systems of others around them, not from what they say they are committed to but how they act. Thus the lack of effective communications had reinforced and supported the divisiveness between team members, and nobody was talking about the reasons why. This supported our "team under the team" that no one deals with (the duck paddles serenely on the surface, but a whole lot of other activity is going on underneath). In addition, this example illustrated how the linkage between task (getting procedures and processes in place) may sometimes conflict with stated values; solving this through effective operational alignment between what we do and how we do it becomes the demonstrable proof that an organization is committed to acting in a certain way.

The next step with this client was to confirm that "what" aspect of moving forward, through a review of the organizational mission and vision. As might be expected, there was no significant change to this, although managers felt that the team was reinforced through having to discuss, clarify, and document their plans. The management team had achieved three things:

1. Started the journey to building more effective relationships with others internally and externally—beginning with knowing self
2. Clarified the core outcomes of the organization in terms of its vision and mission
3. Started to define a set of values that stated the expected individual behavior of those working to achieve the stated outcomes

Points two and three became the basis of communicating expectations to others in the organization, and point one started the work necessary to create leadership that demonstrates a common face and consistent behavior in bringing these commitments to life.

The next stage was to start building a business plan with objectives and outcomes for the next year; having developed the values and created an "is/is not" framework, it became clearer how operational activity would align with organizational behavior. Following completion of this early work, the managers collectively agreed to the outcomes and also to activities necessary to ensure that as this work moved forward, review of and alignment with the stated values would be embedded.

Additional Challenges and Learnings

As we write this book, our efforts with this client remain a work in progress; the team has shown measurable improvements in operating as a cohesive leadership team, with overall scores improving by some 64 percent. In addition, the team is seen by others, including the board, as functioning more effectively and has been able to work through a major strategic shift while remaining reasonably cohesive. The chart shows the shift in the space of twelve months on the twelve questions that were consistently used to assess progress. A key issue here is not just the improvements made but the fact that the impact is measurable. In addition, one can see that while scores have improved, there remain certain key aspects that need work. This indeed is a journey and not an event!

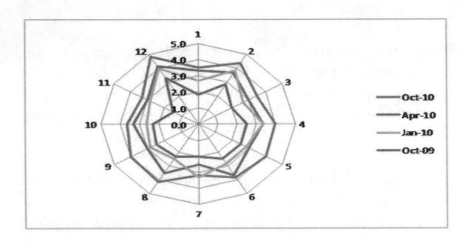

Question Number from chart above	Text of each question
1	There is a strong sense of belonging in our team
2	Team members encourage each other
3	Our meetings are productive
4	We make effective decisions
5	We are able to solve difficult problems
6	We give constructive feedback to each other
7	We openly acknowledge interpersonal conflict
8	Roles and responsibilities are clear
9	Actions result from our team decisions
10	We enjoy each other and have fun together
11	We truly trust each other
12	Team members have the courage of their convictions

Case 3   Public Sector Leadership Team

This leadership team of seven managers requested our assistance to enhance their work as a team and improve their service delivery. The intervention was essentially seen as a developmental opportunity and came out of other work done by the consultant with a number of leadership teams within this particular ministry. As evidenced by the results of the initial *ACT Team Assessment* (see template in appendices) this group was functioning at the "Good" level, with identified areas for improvement. The team met for one day per month for a six-month period (October 2007–March 2008). In addition to this, one-to-one coaching sessions were also built into the program. Each leader completed an emotional-intelligence assessment, and this was used as an aspect of individual leadership development. The results of the intervention demonstrated improvements at both the team and individual levels of functioning. The *ACT* assessment showed a positive movement to the "Excellent" range, and the anecdotal evidence of the participants suggested improvement in overall awareness of leadership style and functioning.

Included in the team's initial objectives were the following:

- To learn techniques to enhance working together
- To work more effectively across units
- To understand strengths and weaknesses
- To learn how to modify behaviors
- To learn how to lead and manage better
- To increase behavior in the next quarter (task and relationship)

In utilizing our Vision, Reality, Action, and Support (VRAS) system (Smyth, 2006), the team identified the following components. (This easy-to-apply model quickly and effectively helps individuals and teams to clarify direction and desired outcomes.)

Components of their *vision* included:

- To solve client problems and to meet their goals
- To be collaborative and also share successes
- To develop a more honest, open, and trusting working environment
- To be excited and to enjoy our workplace

Components of their *reality* included:

- In problem solving, there is too much variation with clients.
- We are improving our collaborative effort.

- We need to restructure HR policies and systems.
- We have a good track record on delivery, but not always in the client's eyes.

Components of their *action* included:

- To be the champions of change
- To develop and execute a plan for areas of improvement with clients
- To change perceptions of clients to being more positive
- To increase recognition and decrease silos

Components of their *support* included:

- To engage clients in a reciprocal and collaborative process
- To have more frequent team and general staff meetings
- To have more regular meetings with clients
- To provide each other with feedback and mutual support

Over the six-month period, improvements were noted in just about all of the areas above. Given the notion that change is indeed a process, the team realized the incremental nature of continuous improvement. Intrateam improvements were noted, particularly in relation to a greater sense of belonging on the team, more productive meetings, and improved decision making. A noticeable improvement was reported in client relations and an improvement in perceptions (both ways!).

Although there was not a dramatic increase in (measurable) team functioning, these leaders acknowledged that they had learned more about themselves and that this allowed them to relate to others more effectively—especially to the people in their own teams as well as their clients, both internal and external.

The team embraced this theme: *A transformed individual is one who can tell the truth; a transformed environment is one in which the truth can be told* (Werner Erhard, from S. Johnson). This theme assisted these leaders in the development of the democratic notion of *power with* others, versus the ubiquitous *power over* others.

A six-month follow-up indicated that, while there was a slight change in team membership due to retirement, the team was essentially on track and continuing in their intended direction.

Case 4   International Pharmaceutical Company: A European Operation

In the spring of 2006, we were invited to facilitate a strategy/ team development project with a major European pharmaceutical company. This was designed as a three-day session, with the senior management committee focusing on strategic goals as well as increasing group cohesion, thereby furthering the development of relationship growth within the committee. The primary purpose was to facilitate the development of this executive committee as a group (later to become a true team). The success of the initial event led to five further three-day sessions over the following four years. All of these off-site sessions took place at various venues in Europe. Planning for each event took place by way of teleconferencing between us, the CEO, and the vice president of personnel.

At the point of our initial involvement, the team could be described as being at the beginning of the second stage of our model of team development. Clearly, this team had moved beyond its initial Formation (stage 1) and was entering into Deliberation (stage 2). Although there may have been some suggestion of ambivalence toward involvement in this new process, there appeared to be merely minor evidence of approach-avoidance behavior in relation to the committee itself and its projects. Observationally, it was clear that this group, with its highly effective leadership, was quite capable of handling the demands of Deliberation.

Most team members had known each other for a few years, although three newer members had been added within the previous year. As indicated earlier in the book, this can act as a positive or a negative dynamic within a team. While some fixed interpersonal perceptions prevailed for this particular group, shifts occurred during our first session as members

175

increasingly gave and received feedback to each other. We used a team-assessment instrument to gauge the effectiveness of the team on such variables as clarity of purpose and objectives; roles and responsibilities; trust and expression of feelings; and decision making and satisfaction with team meetings. We were able to ascertain that this team was already functioning well (actually, above average for teams generally). Typically, this is a direct result of effective team leadership.

Initial ratings on the Team Shamrock were substantially above the general norm (of 2.3) and showed that this team had an excellent foundation for further growth.

(0–5 rating, with 5 being excellent):

- Communication: 3.5
- Collaboration: 3.7
- Coordination: 3.5
- Commitment: 4.3
- Average: 3.75 (75%)

Note: What we have found over the years (and with many teams) is that the average team, at the beginning point of the intervention, scores a 2.3 on the Team Shamrock. This represents 46 percent effectiveness on the four critical aspects. By the Consolidation stage, this team achieved an impressive 4.65 (93 percent) on the Team Shamrock score.

The first event culminated in a two-hour "sharing circle": a facilitated process of giving and receiving feedback with a focus on the quality of interpersonal relationships within the team. Members of this team (as with others teams), called this particular exercise "an unusual and most rewarding experience." The overall success of this visit led to an invitation to facilitate the team's 2007 three-day event. The focus of this was the continuation of the team-development process. A consensus to streamline the team was also arrived at, thereby reducing the membership from sixteen to thirteen. Given the high level of trust and goodwill being established, the process of team membership realignment went very smoothly, as the decision to streamline made sense to the team as a whole.

At the second three-day retreat, the focus was on understanding personality as well as the essential requirements for teamwork. By this time, this executive committee was beginning to feel like an even more effective team and decided to commit to a continuing process with the facilitation of vision, mission, and values in relation to the team's purpose and its overall strategic goals. A team-effectiveness perspective would continue to be the foundation on which future sessions would take place. All of this work was designed, of course, to support the organization's strategic vision and corporate values. Amalgamation (stage 3) had clearly been achieved as the sense of membership, inclusion, and control was shared by all. The quality of regular team meetings (between the off-site sessions) was reported as being high, and there was a corresponding increase in business effectiveness.

In reviewing the results of a previously completed on-line team metric, the team decided that further improvements would occur if they focused on clarifying and developing these four areas for improvement:

- Vision
- Objectives
- Communication
- Trust

Over the following four, three-day sessions, significant improvements would be made in these areas of focus, as well as on all other dimensions of the team's results. Developing a vibrant, shared team vision (based on a clearly articulated set of team values) created the tone for the ongoing work of team development. By now, the team was scoring consistently high on the task-relationship continuum.

In 2008, the team met twice for two further three-day events. The April retreat continued with its team-effectiveness developmental process, and Peter came up with the concept of "guardianship," meaning that each of the team members would agree to assume the role of "Guardian" for various aspects of the team's results as well as the team's values. These guardianships were taken seriously; each member assumed a personal stake in carrying out the task to which they had committed. Furthermore, each participant undertook the task of developing a written mission statement in relation to their particular choice of topic (e.g., the Guardian of Team Personality, the Guardian of Communication, the Guardian of Behavior, the Guardian of Change).

Later, at the September session, each leader made a thirty-minute presentation regarding his or her respective guardianships, which went extremely well, with high-level energy, commitment, and discussion. However, the primary focus of this three-day event was on leadership development with the theme: *What's Love Got to Do with It: Love and Leadership!* This was a truly awe-inspiring happening, as each team member reviewed his or her leadership style in the context of the Love Paradigm, versus the usual and ubiquitous Power Paradigm. (The Love Paradigm, as originally conceptualized by one of our mentors, Professor Norman Goroff, is based on democratic principles and the values of humanistic psychology. In contrast, the Power Paradigm is based on authoritarian principles and the values of individualism and competitiveness.) Erich Fromm's classic, *The Art of Loving*, was recommended by the CEO as required reading for this session.

Adding to the excitement of it all was the team's updated measurement of its results, which continued to reflect both the maintenance and strengthening of its positive developmental direction. The team had indeed reached Consolidation (stage 4) and was clearly (and measurably) functioning as a truly cohesive unit.

In preparation for this particular session, each team member also completed a personal Emotional Intelligence Inventory (EQ-i; Bar-On, 2006). This gave further depth to each leader's self-understanding on fifteen variables ranging from *interpersonal relationship* to *problem solving* to *stress tolerance.* The team-level EQ results were also presented, providing the members with an understanding of their group picture.

In our view, the Bar-On EQ-i is the best researched and comprehensive emotional-intelligence instrument. This easy-to-complete on-line psychometric is designed to measure emotional intelligence in individuals sixteen years of age or older. Emotional intelligence pertains to the emotional, personal, social, and survival dimensions of intelligence, rather than strictly one's ability to learn, recall, think, reason, and abstract. An emotional-intelligence score helps to predict success in life. It also reflects one's current coping skills, one's ability to deal with daily environmental demands, one's degree of common sense, and ultimately, one's overall mental health. From a leadership perspective, we have found this to be an indispensable developmental tool, since one's EQ can be improved.

For our fifth session, in May 2009, the three days began with a review of the results of the team's updated team effectiveness metric. This was followed by each leader providing a one-hour presentation entitled, *My Distinctive Leadership Style.* Using our VRAS model, each leader had organized an amazing presentation on his or her own unique and distinctive style of leadership. Their personal reflections incorporated notes from their personality profile, their EQ results, as well as their leadership profile and their experience. There was an inspiring discussion on how they were applying their learning-to-date with their own divisional/ departmental teams; their presentations reflected how they wanted to be remembered as a leader (their legacy). Their presentations were based on their *personal* values, what made each a distinctive leader, what actions they needed to take to close the gap (between their leadership goals and their current state), how their fellow team members could support them in the realization of their vision, and so on.

As this successful corporation increases its community focus, in its desire to become a truly "patient-centric organization," the team made a memorable afternoon visit to a community-based medical clinic where presentations were made by the medical staff on both community and medical issues. This particular team activity added to the team's overall sense that they were making a real contribution and difference in the world. Furthermore, in the autumn of 2009, this international organization won an award for diversity and inclusion. The notion of inclusion had moved way beyond conception to realization.

In February 2010, this senior management team reconvened for a sixth three-day event. The focus of this retreat was on the application of learning-to-date with *all* of the employee teams within the organization. Directors and leaders had their own teams complete an anonymous on-line team-effectiveness questionnaire, profiling each employee's perception of their specific team. The results were most impressive (and certainly above the norm for organizational teams), showing how every member of the senior management team had internalized and integrated the learning-to-date in leading their own respective teams. At this retreat, the management team members presented a comprehensive overview of how they were actually utilizing their knowledge and skills with the teams they led. As their own leadership capabilities had increased, they now came to collectively understand that inclusion and mutual understanding preceded problem solving and change.

Under the influence of respectful and superb team leadership, this senior corporate team had undoubtedly moved from being a "committee" to being a "team"; they also impressively reached the stage of Consolidation. The stages of Summation and Evaluation would continue on an ongoing basis, thereby completing the circle of the Core Model. Of course, maintaining such positive progress would be an ongoing challenge, especially as alterations in membership and new business demands occur. However, given the team's commitment to values, task, and relationship, as well as the members' consciousness of the importance of communication, collaboration, and effective coordination of effort, a sound foundation had been established on which to move forward successfully into the future. With the addition of indispensable humor, they certainly nurtured a healthy Team Shamrock!

CHAPTER 10

ORGANIZATIONAL THEORY AND LEADERSHIP

An Evolving History

Human behavior and organizational theory are well-established fields of study that are dear to our hearts. Our desire through all of our work has been and continues to be the evolution of this theory as we continue moving forward in this journey we call life. While we may have overlooked some contributions to this field, that was not our desire; however, in the following section, we discuss some of the areas that have had a specific impact on our personal journey and thinking.

The Behavioral Application of Values in Leadership

Over the years, our work has been assisted by a number of theoretical and philosophical frameworks. As with any professional endeavor, the application of principles provides structure and facilitates the implementation (and hopefully the successful completion) of the task or project at hand. Humanistic psychology and social psychology have helped us to understand the essential needs of the person as well as the person in relation to others. We have found that a combined understanding of personality theory and group theory has allowed us to move effectively from principle to practice.

Humanistic psychology aims for a more conscious and humane society. This has guided our holistic approach to the work of helping our clients understand their purpose, meaning, direction, values, and relationships. The humanistic psychological perspective is based on a philosophy of fundamental respect of the dignity, worth, and integrity of all human beings. It is strengths-based and builds on inherent human capacities toward the achievement of personal and group empowerment. A cornerstone of this belief system is consciousness-raising and the development of personal responsibility, without which the concept of self-actualization for the individual, or the group, remains hollow.

Important aspects of social psychology are group theory and social identity theory. These perspectives have direct implications for team and organizational effectiveness. Inclusion, control, and relationship form the basis of the healthy group or team. Feeling included contributes to a sense of identification with the team. Having one's say meets the need for control; and relating effectively to other members builds trust and a strong sense of relationship. A salient aspect of social identity theory is its concern with the psychological aspects of group or team behavior. Put more simply, the more positive the attitudes and behaviors of the leader, as well as the members, the stronger the identification with the team.

Leaders greatly influence the *mood* of the team and the organization. This means that the overall tone and atmosphere within the organizational setting are a reflection of the leader's internal state and behavior. Conscious leaders are mindful of their moods and internal state, and they make behavioral adjustments to ensure that negative feelings are not reactively projected onto others. In other words, one may feel negative emotions without allowing those emotions to dictate one's actual behavior (the difference between *having* anger and the anger *having you*). Acting intentionally is comprised of conscious choices—deliberate behaviors that are intended to induce correspondingly reciprocal behaviors in the other person.

Toward this end, we have employed the Dimensional Model of Human Behavior as an effective behavior-based model in people skills. Lefton and Buzzotta, the cocreators of the model, suggest that the core people skills required of today's managers and leaders are based on "tested common sense" (2004). However, we must acknowledge that sense isn't common to everybody!

The Dimensional Model is based on empirical research and dates back to the late 1940s and 1950s. While we have found its application to be most effective in our personal as well as our professional lives, it is surprising that it has not, apparently, gained much wider notice and attention in the worlds of business and academia. Our corporate clients *always* find it both appealing and usable. In its simplicity, it is profound and allows for self-observation as well as understanding the interpersonal dynamics between self and others. Leaders, as well as personnel at all levels in a wide variety of organizations, have extolled its virtues and its utility. As the reader will see in at least one of our case studies, the Dimensional Model provides measurable outcomes for team development and improvement.

Within the model, four styles of leadership are defined: (1) Autocratic, (2) Unassertive, (3) Easygoing, (4) Collaborative. While it is true that leaders are not necessarily fixated on only one approach, it would seem that managers or leaders essentially gravitate to one of the above styles. And given that we are talking about human behavior, it is also true that we naturally tend to adapt our behavior to the requirements of the situation. However, stress and anxiety play a crucial role in contributing to reactive (vs. proactive or responsive) behavior, and frequently consciousness and intentionality go out the window.

A group of people share a range of qualities and characteristics, which signifies it from other groups. One facet of the group's entity is its emotional characteristics. Just as individuals have moods, emotions, and dispositional affects, groups possess similar attributes that influence aspects such as cohesiveness, performance, and group members. These aspects, in their turn, also influence the group's emotional state (see http:// en.wikipedia.org/wiki/Group_emotion#cite_note-brsd-0).

Group success, like exclusive entry, increases the value of group membership to its members and influences members to identify more strongly with the team and to want to be actively associated with it.

Human development is indeed a journey of understanding, evolution, and occasional revelation; the 2009 book by Jeremy Rifkin[36] placed this journey in a wonderful context; this book presents "a new interpretation of the history of civilization by looking at the empathic evolution of the human race and the

---

[36]   Jeremy Rifkin. *The Empathic Civilization.* Jeremy P. Tarcher/ Penguin Group. 2009.

185

profound ways that it has shaped our development and will likely decide our fate as a species." While these are strong words, they come at a time of great challenge and great opportunity, not just for the practice of leadership but for the way in which this art and science, executed effectively, will have a profound impact on the ability of the human race to move through the challenges of globalization, civil unrest, climate change, and others and come out with an ability to live together in a sustainable way on this small planet we his or her own expertise.

A key to Rifkin's work is the evolving research that shows that contrary to the popular belief that human beings are by nature aggressive and self-interested, we are in fact an empathic species. Based on this, we are in a position to start collaborating, based on a willingness to recognize and practice interdependence, to start resolving the complexities of an interdependent society that has evolved most recently to an incredibly energy-intensive existence that has raised the specter of nonsustainability. Through this, the world is polarized between "haves" and "have nots," even in advanced societies, and as a result, the old styles of leadership (win/lose) and evolving styles of leadership (win/win) constantly clash. It is hard to tell executives today that the style of leadership practiced for the past thirty years (which contributed to their ability to achieve their current salary and status) no longer works.

Another aspect of this type of research is that it reinforces the personal evolutionary journey from being dependent through to codependent, then independent, and finally interdependent. Many individuals reach the third stage but some individuals (and even some societies) tend to promote this as the final stage in development (the image of the Marlboro Man alone on his horse, independent and ready for anything life throws at him—from those who remember the cigarette advertisements of the old days).

Successful personal relationships are built around "you, me, and us"—we retain our individuality but recognize that to successfully be together, we must communicate, collaborate, and cooperate and must approach this in a spirit of commitment; interesting that this mirrors our philosophy in successful group relationships.

We can also consider the work of Erikson and his eight stages of psychological development:

Time of life	Stage	Reinforced	Neglected
Infants: 0–1 year	Hope	Trust	Mistrust
Toddlers: 1–3 years	Will	Autonomy	Shame and doubt
Preschool: 3–6 years	Purpose	Initiative	Guilt
Childhood: 6–12 years	Competence	Industry	Inferiority
Adolescents: 12–18 years	Fidelity	Identity	Role confusion
Young adults: 18–40 years	Love	Intimacy	Isolation
Middle adulthood: 40–65 years	Care	Generativity	Stagnation
Seniors: 65+	Wisdom	Ego integrity	Despair

Successfully passing through these stages will, in all cases, be strongly impacted by the environment within which an individual develops and the way he or she is treated by others and how he or she comes to feel about him or herself as a result. Organizations are groups of individuals coming together as part of their life's journey; Maslow identified in his hierarchy of needs the importance of work itself in developing self-worth—so it is both having a job but also, and critically important, the environment within which one works when one is engaged in the work that either builds or destroys an individual's ability to grow, function effectively, and live a healthy life. The question for leaders then is "What sort of work environment are we creating here?"

This brings us to some more seminal work that we have come to value. First, Stephen Covey's original *Seven Habits of Highly Effective People*, which focused on the individual's role in self-development and our individual ability to change our lives for the better. Covey followed this with *Principle-Centered Leadership*, which really provided the counterpoint to the individual and focused on the role of leaders in creating positive environments. This has impacted our own thinking, especially in the importance of organizations creating a stated set of values that act as a foundation to organizational behavior. Covey generates interesting discussions around the key differences between principles and values, and we support these, but believe that the core concept of organizational values remains critical for success.

While many of these previous writings focused on the human dimension, it is interesting to see that as the science and art of business management has evolved, many authors and experts continually come back to the recognition that "effectiveness of task" cannot be achieved with focusing on the human dimension, which in our philosophy is centered on relationships. Nick's initial business activities, as well as our initial consulting work in the 1990s, were heavily driven by the needs of organizations (employers), and later clients, to address the issues of product and service quality. The work of quality gurus such as Juran, Deming, and Crosby all recognized the criticality of having *both* effective systems and procedures to *manage* processes through which work was done, but equally recognized that *without human engagement and commitment,* such efforts would be suboptimal. Our experience clearly demonstrated this with clients who wanted a quality system implemented to manage process but deployed it in such a way that staff saw it as just another program. We enjoyed the writing of Donald Peterson,[37] CEO of Ford Motor Company, whose book illustrated the different road that Ford chose to take in the 1970s when quality and cost were key issues in the automotive business. While others spent billions on automation, Ford worked harder to engage with its employees and have them be part of the solution. This is one reason that we still like Deming's fourteen points. In other areas of process management, we again see this focus on starting with task and realizing that without the human dimension, improvement will probably not happen. *Reengineering the Corporation*[38] *was quickly followed by James Champy's Reengineering Management.*

The bottom line is that management theory, in particular around leadership, as well as the professions of sociology and psychology, have been developing for years, and much of what we are trying to do today is to manage change and apply these learnings to the behavior of people within group settings—in particular, in the role of leadership. Leadership is like any other profession: while many areas of skills and knowledge can be learned, the underlying foundation is that of a "calling" to be instrumental in making the world a better place for those who live in it. Too often today, leaders are attracted and retained by the financial aspects of the job rather than by a desire to focus on the humanistic aspects

---

[37] Donald E. Peterson. *A Better Way*. Houghton-Mifflin. 1991.

[38] Michael Hammer and James Champy. *Reengineering the Corporation*. Harper Collins. 1993.

of the role. Effective leaders must have an aspect of love in what they do; recently, we had the opportunity to work with Janice Mae Parviainen, who inspires leaders and others she comes into contact with. She further emphasized this aspect of true leadership. Janice's calling has come from a place of love, which guides her commitment to make this world a better place. Her workshops and book *Courage to Love Yourself*[39] *are an essential foundation of leading others and provide a springboard from which all of us can leap to a better place.*

The Use of Psychometric Assessments

We have discussed a number of times in this book the importance of leaders (and, in fact, all of us) starting their development journey by knowing themselves better. We are unique, fascinating, and complex individuals formed by a combination of attributes we were born with plus those that developed during our life experiences and the stages of our personal growth to date. Those involved with a stronger belief of the spiritual aspects of the human soul will also add to this the attributes that we bring from our spirits and souls and their previous experiences. While there is no right or wrong, pass or fail template for the human condition, we each can enhance our journey by a reflective assessment of our own personality traits and behavioral preferences.

We use a number of assessment tools in our work for understanding where individuals and teams are in areas such as communications and conflict resolution; identifying where organizations are in terms of knowing and applying corporate values and ethics; and knowing to what degree each of us as individuals believes that we are task

---

[39]   Janice Mae Parviainen. *Courage to Love Yourself.* JMP Consultants. 2009.

versus relationship oriented (and also asking others who work with us what they think). We also use tools such as emotional-intelligence assessment to help us work with others and understand approaches to individual interactions. However, core to our work has been the use of psychometric tools based on the work of Carl Jung that adopt the concept of four colors that help express individual preferences and, from this, help us understand behavior and interactions with others. There are many excellent tools available in the marketplace, many of which are available in many languages and validated across a broad range of different cultures.

A fairly recent tool is Lumina Learning's Spark portrait; this product is the evolutionary development of extensive career work by Stewart Desson. This product is one of a family of offerings that help us with consulting interventions, through which we help transform organizations by developing the human dimension. We particularly like this latest approach, because it moves beyond the traditional core Jungian measures of introvert or extrovert; feeling or thinking; intuition or sensing; and judging or perceiving. Lumina provides a clear portrait of an individual that starts with the four color energies of red, yellow, blue, and green and then develops these into eight aspects and twenty-four individual qualities. These twenty-four behavioral aspects are then presented in three personas of the underlying (unscripted) you; the everyday (scripted) you; and, finally, the overextended you (typically, where we go under stress). While all three personas provide a valuable understanding of self, the overextended you adds a key dimension to understanding individuals and teamwork; in today's environment, many managers spend much of their time in this place. Many clients who have experience with other psychometrics say that Lumina provides a very realistic assessment of themselves and the others that they know.

Call to Action: Summary of Next Steps

This book provides a framework for understanding and improving leadership effectiveness, but many clients want to cut to the chase and ask, "So what do I actually have to do?" This short section is for those who have read through the material and now want a quick summary. But a word of caution! Throughout this book, we have repeatedly stressed that successful cultures are not built overnight, nor are they sustained by a mechanical program or approach. Here are the building blocks for organizational success built around leadership that creates and builds effective relationships as an enabler of organizational success:

Checklist for moving forward (Note: NI means "Needs Improvement")

#	Question	Yes	No	NI	Action plan
	VALUES, VISION, AND MISSION				
	Are your organizational values clearly defined and written down?				
	Is there a clear mission and vision?				
	Do these clearly reflect the views of all the key stakeholders of the organization?				
	Are these three factors (Vision, Values, and Mission—V2M) core to hiring policy?				
	Has the organization clearly defined "Do/Do Not" expectations to support values?				
	Have all those in leadership positions affirmed and committed to the values?				

#	Question	Yes	No	NI	Action plan
	Are the key factors built in to orientation programs?				
	Are the key factors a part of all leadership training?				
	Are managers assessed on both what they do (outcomes) as well as how they do it compared to stated expectations (values)?				
	LEADERSHIP DEVELOPMENT				
	Have all individuals in leadership positions been selected for both management and leadership skills (are competency requirements in place)?				
	Have all people in leadership positions been helped in their development by a psychometric assessment and feedback?				
	Is updating leadership skills a part of all managers' development plans?				
	Do managers discuss with their staff mutual success in living the values?				
	Are managers developed through changing exposure to new teams and personalities?				
	LIVING THE VALUES				
	Are aspects of living the values embedded in key business processes?				
	Does the enterprise risk assessment identify key areas where practice of the values may be exposed?				
	Have all policies and procedures been cross-referenced to the values (i.e., correlated?)				

#	Question	Yes	No	NI	Action plan
	Have all HR policies and procedures in particular been validated to ensure alignment with values?				
	Are rewards and recognition systems consistent with living the values?				
	MEASURING PERFORMANCE				
	Are metrics in place to assess leadership effectiveness?				
	Is regular feedback from clients on organizational behavior in place?				
	Do supplier reviews include aspects of relationship management?				
	Do employees have the opportunity to assess and feedback managers "living the values"?				
	Are key areas, such as effective communications, tracked and monitored on a regular basis?				

This list provides an example of some of the concepts included in this book that help lay a solid foundation for an organization that balances both task achievement and relationship management. As a final reflection, the following chart identifies the highlights of establishing and building a framework for organizational values upon which effective leadership and relationship building rests.

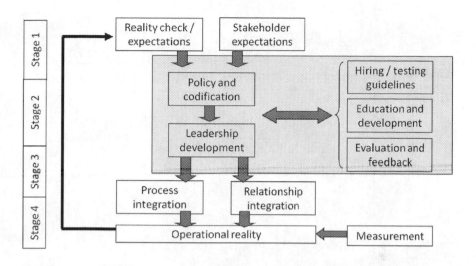

Step by step, built on a foundation of knowing who we are, what we stand for, and what we are trying to achieve, organizations, composed of the collective efforts of many individuals, can move forward. The foundation is vision, mission, and values from which organizational culture is built. Upon this foundation stand the core components of turning intent into reality—the people and processes, internally and externally. Finally, sustainability for the future rests on the culture encouraging continual searching for improvement in every single aspect of organizational activity by every single member of the team. Great things are achieved by groups of ordinary people who are motivated and committed. These are not superstars but individuals who feel valued and who are passionate about doing what they do every day.

APPENDICES

EXAMPLES AND TEMPLATES

BACKGROUND ON THE AUTHORS

NICK A. SHEPHERD, FCMC; FCGA; FCCA; FCMI
Certified Management Consultant
President, EduVision Inc.

Nick A. Shepherd has more than forty years of business experience, and since 1989, he has been running his own management-consulting and professional-development company, EduVision Inc., which provides professional facilitation and management-consulting and development services to public and private sector organizations.

Nick is a fellow of the Institute of Certified Management Consultants of Ontario (FCMC, Honor Roll) and past president of the Institute; he is also past chair of the National Certification Committee for all Institutes of Management Consulting across Canada and past chair of the Professional Standards Committee of the International Council of Management Consulting Institutes (ICMCI), and he served as one of four trustees for Canada at the ICMCI. Nick has been a certified general accountant for over thirty years and is a fellow of the Chartered Association of Certified Accountants (FCCA UK) and the Chartered Management Institute (FCMI UK). Nick is a senior member of the American Society for Quality and past chair of the Quality Costs Committee of the Management Quality Division. He is also a member of Mensa.

Nick is a well-known professional-development facilitator and teaches three-day "Controllers Programs" and two-day "Advanced Controllers Programs"; Nick also presents many professional-development workshops across Canada on an annual basis. In 2006, Nick received the President's Award for Education from the Certified General Accountants of British Columbia.

Nick is the author of *Governance, Accountability, and Sustainable Development* (published by Thomson Carswell), which deals with governance issues for the twenty-first century, and *Controller's Handbook* (now in its second edition); these are just two of the books and articles that Nick has written. Nick was one of a group of global contributors to the International Federation of Accountants (IFAC) report on sustainability entitled *Professional Accountants in Business—At the Heart of Sustainability*. Nick has also authored the publications *Values and Ethics: From Inception to Practice,*

The Evolution of Accountability—Sustainability Reporting for Accountants, and a new publication, *Unrecognized Intangible Assets: Identification, Management, and Reporting,* published by the US Institute of Management Accountants. Nick has also developed several ethics courses for members and students of the Certified General Accountants and for management-consulting institutes.

PETER SMYTH, MScEd, MSW, PhD, (C) OACCPP
Senior Consultant EduVision Inc., and Director of
THE COUNSELING INSTITUTE.

Peter J. Smyth has over thirty years of experience in the fields of mental health, adult education, and organizational consultation. He holds numerous qualifications in the various areas of group work, leadership, coaching, emotional intelligence, personal and group assessment, communication, and problem solving. He is accredited in the administration and facilitation of the globally recognized Lumina Learning systems. Peter is a senior consultant with EduVision Inc., through which he brings his skills to the assistance of a wide range of corporate clients.

Peter is the director of the Counseling Institute in Woodbridge, Ontario, where he practices relational psychotherapy and executive coaching. He has been a professor at York University for the past twenty-seven years and has taught at three other universities. As a corporate coach and consultant, Peter has worked with a wide variety of organizations in both the private and public sectors, and he also provides consultancy services to a number of health-care and educational institutions. He is committed to personal and cultural transformation through the development of consciously collaborative environments that are motivational and responsive to both human and organizational needs for growth.

In addition to his extensive private sector experience, Peter has had a long professional relationship with the public sector, including the Ontario Government. Over the past twelve years he has worked with the Ontario Public Service and various Ministries and Departments. He spent seven years on the faculty of the Centre for Leadership and Learning, Cabinet Office, for the Senior Leadership Development Program. He continues to be on the faculty of the Centre of Excellence in Critical Care Medicine (Mount Sinai/University of Toronto) and was also an active member of the Teamwork and Leadership Critical Care Coaching Team (MOHLTC Critical Care Secretariat).

Peter has written numerous articles in the areas of psychology and group work. He brings both wit and wisdom to his work.

Examples of Joint Consulting Projects

- Developed and jointly facilitated executive workshops for senior managers in the implementation of TQM, focusing on behavioral aspects of change management.

- Worked with a number of clients on team-development activities, using psychometric methodology as a tool for executive and team development, including both public and private sector organizations, from small- to medium-sized enterprises (SMEs) to multinational organizations.

- Conducted a pre-implementation assessment at the maintenance facilities of a major international airline, to assess alignment and consistency between stated commitment to quality and alignment with people strategies within the organization.

- Conducted a national assessment of a major computer services company (revenues in excess of $1B) to evaluate management, supervisory, and employee alignment with company goals and objectives.

- Designed, developed, and implemented human-resources surveys to identify issues related to communications both among executive team members and between managers and all other staff; results were analyzed and communicated and changes made to HR strategy.

- Conducted team-development activities at executive level for a major US manufacturer, initially with the operations management team in Canada and then in Atlanta, Georgia.

- Worked with the general manager of a privately owned business in developing a management team of an existing business unit, changing management style from hierarchical to participative; results included company achieving profitability and continuing to be a star performer in the group.

- Conducted a benchmarking comparison of five Canadian facilities of a major US corporation (approximately $12B in sales at the time) to assess root causes for differences in plant productivity and operational effectiveness; success achieved when core causes were identified and validated.

- Worked with executive team of a major privately held family business with global operations, to assist in third-generation transition; developed and assisted in deployment of organizational vision and values; and supported executive team in addressing challenges with consistent application of stated values.

- Ongoing executive team support for a major division of the above family business with operations in Canada, Mexico, Australia, Germany, Holland, and the UK, including joint facilitation of annual global retreats in Mexico, Canada, and Los Angeles (work includes coaching and support of individual managers between each group retreat).

- Coordination of work with the above client in executive development with managers of seven US operations including assessments of managers and team facilitations.

- Extension of work with family-owned business to now include all global operations in Europe, North and South America, and Asia.

- Developed a complete curriculum for certification of managers in public sector service delivery area.

- Developed leadership-development workshop for a leading institute supported by federal, provincial, and local governments, targeted for managers in the public sector service delivery arena including psychometric assessment.

The RP5 Management Model of Excellence

This model has been developed as part of our ongoing desire to embrace past research into organizational excellence yet bring a greater balance to the outcome (task) and relationship aspects. While this is a work in progress, it does allow for a high level of alignment with many well-established models.

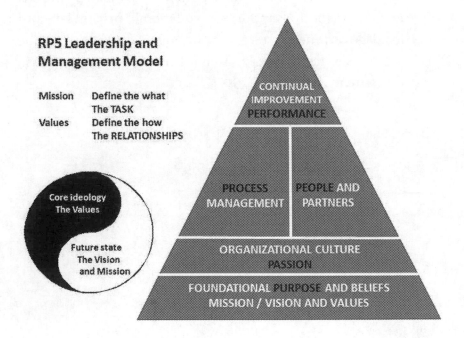

Further explanations of RP5 as well as outlines of the "5 Ps" are shown below:

Leader is Reflective	Reflective of self as well as organizational capacity, capability, and execution	Self-aware; seeks input; knows personal strengths and areas to seek help and support. Challenges organizational status quo; works with facts; engages and shares
Leader focuses on 5Ps	Purpose	Engages in organizational vision, mission, and values and translates intent into action; clear under-standing of foundations of the organization's intent and direction; understands critical balance of task and relationships
	Passion	Guardian of the organizational values in practice; driven by commitment to serve and perform; has a passion for engaging others and following the vision, mission, and values; able to "work the system" to constantly improve all aspects of work
	People	Stimulated by the challenge of engaging the workforce as a team to convert plans into action; energized by the diversity of human nature and behavior; exercises power through people not over people; seeks to enable success and serve
	Process	Understands importance of defined process but able to focus on "doing what makes sense" and challenging status quo; willing to take risk to try new approaches; encourages staff to "go the extra mile"; views process from perspective of client in areas such customer/client focus, quality, and satisfaction

	Performance	Understands need for effective outcomes and clear accountability; holds self accountable for unit's performance; seeks and uses "fact-based management"; shares information with others; seeks constant improvement in all areas of effectiveness
Knows impor-tance of "5"	Driven to achieve highest levels of per-formance	5/5 rating in satisfaction as the goal: "5 out of 5 is where we strive" Understands the five drivers of organizational success: purpose, passion, people, process, and performance Builds leadership on 5Ps of effective management

ACT Team Assessment

This is a tool that is used at the beginning and during team-development activity in order to assess progress. Typically we plot changes on a radar graph that depicts the progress of the team. This ranges from 50 percent improvement to over a doubling of performance. The two key metrics are the overall average/median score for the team in question and the range spread of the cores. Each tells us different information indicating different intervention requirements.

ACT Team Assessment

The following brief survey will help assess the level at which the team is currently operating; please answer based on your best personal assessment rather than what you think others may answer.

	Please rate the following as 1–5 (1 being low and 5 being high)					
1	There is a strong sense of belonging in our team	1	2	3	4	5
2	Team members encourage each other	1	2	3	4	5
3	Our meetings are productive	1	2	3	4	5
4	We make effective decisions	1	2	3	4	5
5	We are able to solve difficult problems	1	2	3	4	5
6	We give constructive feedback to each other	1	2	3	4	5
7	We openly acknowledge interpersonal conflict	1	2	3	4	5
8	Roles and responsibilities are clear	1	2	3	4	5
9	Actions result from our team decisions	1	2	3	4	5
10	We enjoy each other and have fun together	1	2	3	4	5
11	We truly trust each other	1	2	3	4	5
12	Team members have the courage of their convictions	1	2	3	4	5

Overall team score			Range	
48–60	Excellent			
36–47	Fair/Good			
24–35	Poor; Must Improve			
12–23	Help Needed			

Results of ACT Assessment in Practice

The ACT assessment outlined above as a template is used as a core instrument to assess objectively the progress that a team makes over a period of intervention. This example from one of our previous case studies demonstrates considerable progress. However, while it can be pleasing to "pat oneself on the back" for improvements, there remain underlying issues as some key aspects of team improvement remain low.

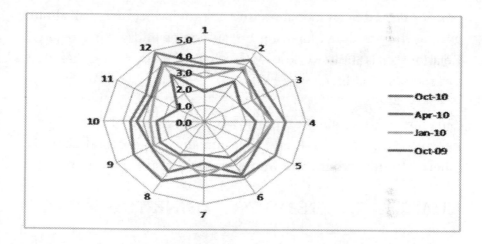

Nevertheless, such a depiction of progress does help to identify movement in team interaction; the challenge is to ensure that this "relationship building" is translating into greater task effectiveness. This is where operational metrics need to be added to the mix. The question "How are we actually doing our task aspects more effectively?" needs to be answered.

Example of Survey of Individual and 360-degree Task/Relationship Assessment

Name _____

Department/Team _____

This survey is designed to assess the level of focus on *tasks and relationships* that an individual and a team have. (Task is all about getting the job done, focusing on outcomes and getting results. Relationship is about working with others and developing effective interpersonal skills.)

This first chart will be your own assessment of where you *personally* score in Task and Relationship. The second chart is where you think your team would score (overall) as a group.

CHART 1 WHERE DO YOU THINK YOU SCORE?

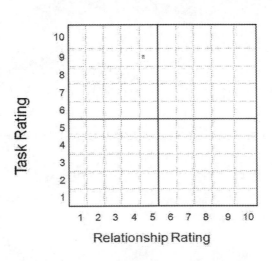

On this chart, show what your *personal* ranking would be on a scale of 1–10 (1 being very low and 10 being very high) for your "task" orientation and your "relationship" orientation (i.e., where you think you operate).

(As an example, someone who felt he or she was 9 on "task" and 5 on "relationship" would plot his or her result where the "E" is shown.)

CHART 2   WHERE DO YOU THINK YOUR TEAM SCORES?

Now show on this chart where you think the overall team that you work with would show up in their "task" and "relationship" results. Remember, this is *your* opinion of where the team is functioning.

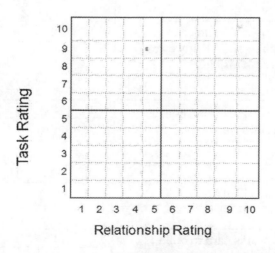

There is no wrong or correct score, no "pass" or "fail" from these results; they provide information that will help you and your team identify any potential areas for working together more effectively and improving your effectiveness.

Values Evaluation and Assessment

The following is an extract from a brief survey designed as a self-assessment for managers. It should be reviewed on a regular basis and used to identify opportunities for improvement. When used in conjunction with an employee assessment, it may identify possible gaps between managers' assessments of their leadership approach and what other employees actually perceive.

Please rate your agreement with these comments on a scale of 1–5 (1=strongly disagree, 5=strongly agree)

Think about the questions as all starting with the words "I believe that . . ."	Strongly disagree	Disagree	Not clear/no opinion	Agree	Strongly agree
1. The decisions we make and actions we take as a business show that we are environmentally responsible.	1	2	3	4	5
2. I believe that we operate and behave as an ethical organization.	1	2	3	4	5
3. Our company generates value in its dealings with clients.	1	2	3	4	5
4. Our company works hard to build "win/win" relationships with clients and to understand their business needs.	1	2	3	4	5
5. We are seen as a leader in technology.	1	2	3	4	5

6. We strongly support and foster technology cooperation and sharing where possible.	1	2	3	4	5

7. We encourage employee innovation and encourage and apply employee ideas.	1	2	3	4	5

Application Note:

In developing a survey such as this, the starting point is the statement of values; these are then turned around into questions that are used to validate behavior.

Assessment of Commitment to Values
by Managers during Development

The following table is used as a basis for discussion when values have been initially developed, and the next stage has been reached during which manager or leader buy-in becomes critical.

Value (statement):						
Are you, as a leader, willing to:	Strongly disagree	Disagree	No opinion	Agree	Strongly agree	Actions and suggestions
Agree with this value as an overall concept?						
Freely accept this value personally?						
Publicly affirm this value through your behavior?						
Prize and cherish this value (care about it)?						
Act on this value consistently?						

Typically, this is a process that takes some time as leaders develop a commitment to the values that they are prepared to uphold. Creating this chart develops a good basis for discussion, and it is often used in conjunction with the following example of an "Is/Is Not" assessment that determines what behavior would demonstrate commitment to the values. Again, this tends to be an ongoing learning process.

Example of a Developing Definition to Understand the Stated Value

This document is used to assist in developing an understanding by managers and leaders of the type of behavior that might exist to demonstrate alignment with the values in day-to-day activities. This is important, as many organizations fail the "values credibility test" because the daily activities do not support and reflect the stated values.

Stated Value = "To be Environmentally Responsible"	
What this means	**What we would NOT be doing**
❑ To be fully compliant with regulations and laws	❑ Doing the minimum necessary
❑ To be registered to a recognized international or national standard	❑ Circumventing the proper use of equipment
❑ To conduct internal checks and audits to ensure compliance	
❑ To have systems in place, as an example for testing for compliance	
❑ To have $0 fines and penalties	
❑ To receive no negative notifications from any inspection or compliance body	
❑ To use the best appropriate and available technology	
❑ To be seen as proactive through applying best practices, training staff, and sharing experience within the group	

Creation of the "Is/Is Not" document should be a participative activity both at the leadership level as well as during deployment of values.

The GROWS Framework

The GROWS action-planning approach reflects the learning from the Lumina Spark portrait and is one of the many learning and development interventions that can come from such a rich psychometric assessment process.

The following chart identifies how four out of the five steps in the process link back to the use of particular color energies.

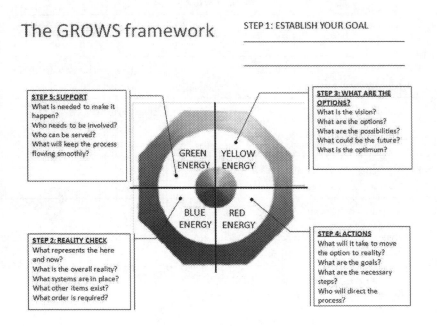

The GROWS framework

STEP 1: ESTABLISH YOUR GOAL

STEP 5: SUPPORT
What is needed to make it happen?
Who needs to be involved?
Who can be served?
What will keep the process flowing smoothly?

STEP 3: WHAT ARE THE OPTIONS?
What is the vision?
What are the options?
What are the possibilities?
What could be the future?
What is the optimum?

GREEN ENERGY YELLOW ENERGY

BLUE ENERGY RED ENERGY

STEP 2: REALITY CHECK
What represents the here and now?
What is the overall reality?
What systems are in place?
What other items exist?
What order is required?

STEP 4: ACTIONS
What will it take to move the option to reality?
What are the goals?
What are the necessary steps?
Who will direct the process?

Using this process both individuals and teams can map a plan to move forward and apply specific personal and team learning and, through this, gradually enhance performance.

The Answer to the Dots . . .

As in so many of these puzzles, the answer requires thinking outside the box; in this case, particularly, as we would traditionally be bound by the apparent square within which the dots are created; however, if we go beyond the boundaries, we can solve the problem!

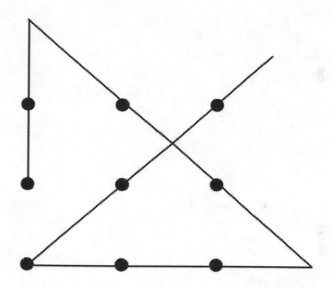

Thanks to an unknown anonymous source for this puzzle; it just proves once again that there are many, many creative people in this world.

BIBLIOGRAPHY

Adams, M., and M. Oleksak. (2010). *Intangible Capital.* Santa Barbara, CA: Praeger.

Aguayo, R. (1990). *Dr. Deming: The American Who Taught the Japanese About Quality.* New York: Fireside Books by Simon & Schuster.

Akao, J. (1991). *Hoshin Kanri.* Cambridge, MA: Productivity Press.

Anderson, D. (2010). *Design for Manufacturability & Concurrent Engineering.* Cambria, CA: CIM Press.

Bar-On, R. (2006). *Bar-On Emotional Quotient Inventory (EQ-i).* Toronto: Multi Health Systems.

Berry, L. L. (1999). *Discovering the Soul of Service.* New York: The Free Press/Simon & Schuster.

Blanchard, K., and N. V. Peale. (1988). *The Power of Ethical Management.* New York: Fawcett Crest Books by Ballantine.

Brand Finance. (2009). *Intangible Finance Tracker.* London: Brand Finance.

Brimson, J. A. (1994). *Activity-Based Management*. New York: Wiley.

Buckingham, M., and C. Coffman. (1999). *First, Break All the Rules: What the World's Greatest Managers Do Differently*. New York: Simon & Schuster.

Buzzotta, Lefton, and Sherberg. *Effective Selling Through Psychology: The Dimensional Sales Model*. New York: Wiley. 1972

Buzzotta, V. R., and R. E. Lefton. (2005). *Dimensional Selling*. New York: McGraw-Hill.

Carlzon, J. (1987). *Moments of Truth*. London: Harper Perennial.

Collection. (2005). *The Lean Office*. New York: Productivity Press.

Collins, J. C. (1994). *Built to Last*. New York: Harper Collins.

Cooper, K. M., R. S. Kaplan, and L. S. Maisel. (1993). *Implementing Activity-Based Cost Management*. Montvale, NJ: Institute of Management Accountants.

Covey, S. (1989). *The Seven Habits of Highly Effective People*. New York: Fireside Books by Simon & Schuster.

Covey, S. (1990/1991). *Principle-Centered Leadership*. New York: Summit Books, Simon & Schuster.

Covey, S., R. A. Merrill, and R. R. Merrill. (1994). *First Things First*. New York: Simon & Schuster.

Deming, Dr. W. E. (2000). *Out of Crisis.* Cambridge, MA: MIT Press.

Edvinsson, L. (1997). *Intellectual Capital.* New York: Harper Business.

Frank, J. J. (1951). *Juran's Quality Control Handbook.* New York: McGraw-Hill.

Fromm, E. (2006). *The Art of Loving.* New York: Harper Perennial.

Goroff, N. (1982). "The Social Construction of the Feeling of Personal Inadequacy: An Aspect of Social Control." West Hartford: University of Connecticut (unpublished).

Hand, J., and B. Lev, eds. (2003). *Intangible Assets.* Oxford: Oxford University Press.

Harry, M. (2000). *Six Sigma.* New York: Doubleday.

Havard, A. (2007). *Virtuous Leadership.* New York: Scepter Publishers.

Interview. (2010). *"Under the Hood at Toyota's Recall."* Knowledge@ Wharton 3.

Johnson, S. (1987). *Humanizing the Narcissistic Style.* New York: W.W. Norton.

Kaplan, R. S. (1996). *The Balanced Scorecard.* Boston: Harvard Business Press.

Kaplan, R. S., and D. P. Norton. (2008). *The Execution Premium.* Boston: Harvard Business Press.

Ken, B. (2007). *Leading at a Higher Level.* Upper Saddle River, NJ: Prentice Hall.

Lefton, R.E. and V. R. Buzzotta. (2004). *Leadership through People Skills.* Toronto: McGraw-Hill.

Lewin, K. (1951) *Field Theory in Social Science: Selected Theoretical Papers.* D. Cartwright (ed.). New York: Harper & Row

Liker, J. K. (2004). *The Toyota Way.* New York: McGraw-Hill.

Luft, J. (1969). *Of Human Interaction.* Palo Alta, CA: National Press.

Mahoney, F. X. (1994). *The TQM Trilogy.* New York: AMACOM.

Mortenson, G., and D. Relin. (2007). *Three Cups of Tea.* New York: Penguin.

Peterson, D. E. (1991) *A Better Way.* Boston: Houghton Mifflin.

Peters, T. (1982). *In Search of Excellence.* New York: Harper & Row.

Peters, T. (1985). *A Passion for Excellence.* New York: Random House.

Rifkin, J. (2009). *The Empathic Civilization.* New York: Jeremy P. Tarcher/Penguin Group.

Shepherd, N. (2005). *Governance, Accountability, and Sustainable Development: An Agenda for the 21ˢᵗ Century.* Toronto: Carswell Thomson.

Shepherd, N. (2008). *Controller's Handbook,* 2nd edition. Toronto, Canada: CCH Canadian Division of Wolters Kluwer.

Shepherd, N. (2008). *The Evolution of Accountability: Sustainability Reporting for Accountants.* Montvale, NJ: Institute of Management Accountants.

Shepherd, N. (2008). *Values and Ethics: From Inception to Practice.* Montvale, NJ: Institute of Management Accountants.

Shepherd, N. (2010). *Unrecognized Intangible Assets: Identification, Management, and Reporting.* Montvale, NJ: Institute of Management Accountants.

Simon, S., H. Kirchenbaum, and H. Leland. (1995). *Values Clarification.* New York: Hart Publishing.

Smyth, P. J. (1991). "Hope: A Fundamental Issue in Humanistic Social Work with Groups." *Social Science Journal, Annual Edition* 4–10.

Smyth, P. J. (2006). "Understanding Yourself and Others." In *The Leadership Guide for Healthcare Professionals,* T. E. Stewart and C. Mazza, eds. Oakville, ON: J. Hylands and Associates.

Smyth, P. J. (2009). "A Phenomenological Typology of Narcissism." *Psychologica* Spring, 4–8. eds. pp. 108-124.

Stewart, T. A. (1997). *Intellectual Capital: The New Wealth of Organizations*. New York: Currency Books by Doubleday.

Sveiby, K. E. (1997). *The New Organziational Wealth*. San Francisco: Berrett-Koehler.

Walton, M. (1986). *The Deming Management Method*. New York: Perigee Books, Putnam.

Watzlawick, P. (1978). *The Language of Change: Elements of Therapeutic Communication*. New York: W.W. Norton.

INDEX

Page numbers with *italic "n"* reference footnote entries
Page numbers with *italic "ill"* reference illustrations, charts, graphics, tables and checklists

ABEF (Australian Business Excellence Framework) criteria, 36*ill*, 116
accountability, 25, 145, 158, 210
acknowledgment, 64, 89, 100, 103
ACT Team Assessment tool, 171, 172, 211–217
activity perspective, 156
Activity-Based Costing (ABC), 34, 41
Activity-Based Management (Brimson), 34, 224
Adams, Mary, 8, 8*n*, 165*ill*, 223
Adler, Alfred, 69
administration, 41
administrative information, 37
affiliation, 67

Afghanistan, 24
Africa, xiv
agile organizations, 131, 145
aging population, 31
agreement, 43, 100, 108
Aguayo, B., 223
"Ah ha" moment, 3
Akao, Yoji, 21, 25*n*, 25*n*9, 223
Alaska, 163
alienation, 67, 86
alignment
    of business strategy and vales, 53
    of defined values, 57
    effective operational, 169
    in evaluations, of performance, 131
    human resource management, 52

leading to organizational
effectiveness, 118
of relationships, 124
of stakeholder interests,
121
with stock holder interests,
121
between the
Task-Relationship Model
and an organizational HR
strategy, 130
allocation of resources, 20,
31, 143
amalgamation stage, 81,
89–90, 160, 177
American Management
Association (AMA),
44–45, 44n
American Society for Quality
(ASQ), 32, 33
Anderson, David M., 27, 27n,
143, 143n, 223
approach-avoidance, 83
Aristotle, 63
Art of Loving (Fromm),
179, 225
Asia, xiv, 24, 44
as-if team, 97–101
ASQ (American Society for
Quality), 32, 33
assertiveness and action, 101
assessment
of commitment to values,
218

completed EQ, 155
emotional-intelligence,
171, 191
objective, 50
psychometric, 155,
158, 190–191
reflective, 190
assets
intangible, 19, 23, 27,
53, 121, 129
nontangible, 38
people as, 128, 129–130
tangible, 8, 9ill, 14, 19, 20
attitudes, behavior and
positive, 183
Aurelius, Marcus, 106
Australia, 35–36
Australian Business Excellence
Framework (ABEF)
criteria, 36ill, 116
authoritarian leaders, 73
authoritarian principles, 179
authority, delegation of, 142
autocratic leaders, 89, 158, 185
awards for excellence, 35, 36ill
awareness
conscious, 60, 61, 83
of culture of collaboration,
74
facilitating, 88
of followers, 64
intuitive, 79
lack of, 63
of need for inclusion and

acceptance, 84
of values, 82, 83

Bagehot, Walter, 102
balance
connection creating, 91
of internal controls and
level of controls, 54
between outcomes and
behavior, 142, 142*ill*
of task and relationships,
65, 68, 71, 100, 142, 209
Balanced Scorecard, 34, 147,
152–153
The Balanced Scorecard
(Kaplan and Norton), 152*n*,
225
Baldrige Award, 8, 25, 35, 36*ill*,
116
Barings Bank, 144
Barnes, Jonathan, 63, 63*n*
Bar-On, R, 179, 223
*Bar-On Emotional Quotient
Inventory* (Bar-On), 179,
223
barriers, to effective
communication, 110–112
Beauvoir, Simone de, xiii, xvi
behavior
antiteam, 76
approach-avoidance, 175
balance between outcomes
and, 142
concentrating on shared
mission and, 132
corporate ethics and, 13
customer-focused, 132
in developing
high-performing teams, 73
dissonance between
declarations and, 99
dominant-hostile, 111
dominant-warm quadrant
of, 112
embracing task and, 53
expectation af leaders, 70
expectation of
organizational, 46
harmful interpersonal, 63
internal controls and, 146
leaders attitudes and, 61,
82
leader's values/philosophy
and, 69
mirroring corporate
direction, 146
mission and, 149
organizational, 141,
165, 169
setting direction for, 119
sharing common goals and,
113
stress and anxiety influence
on, 185
translating statement into,
133

understanding, 191
values and, 49, 118, 125, 168
behavioral application of values in leadership, 182–190
behavior-based model, effective, 184
beliefs
in human soul, 190
values and, 103, 166
values statements and, 56
Ben & Jerrys, 12
Bend It Like Beckham (movie), 45
Benjamin, Alan, 19
Berry, L. L., 48, 223
A Better Way (Peterson), 85*n*22, 189, 189*n*37, 226
Blanchard, Ken, 21, 22, 223
board of directors
creating self-assessment programs for improvement, 59
focused on measuring tasks, 148
link to organizational values, 54
role of, 56
selection of link to management, 57, 58
setting stage of expectations, 119
working with, 95
Body Shop, 12

book value
vs. historical value, 12, 155
vs. market valuation, 7
Bowlby, John, 91
BPC Generation Infrastructure Trust, 55
BPR (Business Process Reengineering), 17, 26, 138
Brand Finance, 7*ill*, 223
Brimson, J. A., 34, 224
British Chartered Management Institute, 127
British Columbia, 163
broad-based performance-measurement system, 153
Buber, Martin, 64
Buckingham, Marcus, 130, 130*n*, 224
building blocks, in developing effective relationships, 168
Build-to-Order & Mass Customization (Anderson), 143, 143*n*
Built to Last (Collins), 34, 224
business
intelligence, core, 135
management, 35, 188
mission and vision, 120
planning, 21, 123, 158
process optimization, xiv
business effectiveness, increasing, 177

business environment,
    changing, 6–13
business expansion, and
    development, 38
Business Process
    Reengineering (BPR), 17,
    26, 138
buy-in
    actual, 109
    building, 110
    to compliance, 145
    increasing, 84, 105, 107
    of leaders vision, 74
Buzzotta, Victor R., 21*n*, 111,
    224, 226

Cadbury Commission, 144
call to action, 192–195
Cameco Corporation, 55
Canada, 10, 35–36, 43, 44, 54,
    116, 136
Canadian Awards for
    Excellence, 116
Canadian Awards for
    Excellence (NQI) criteria,
    36*ill*, 116
capability, motivation and, 129
capacity
    applying innovation and
    creativity, 149
    assessing organizational, 23
    excess, 30

of humanistic leaders, 67
    organizational, 148, 149,
    209
Carlzon, Jan, 8, 134, 140, 224
Cartwright, 108, 226
Cartwright, D., 108*n*
Champy, James, 189, 189*n*38
change
    focusing on behavioral, 12
    handling, 163
    holistic approaches to, 36
    impact on values and, 125
    involving people in, 137,
    138
    lasting, 27
    leadership and, 101–109,
    108*ill*
    long-term, 24
    of management control, 25
    management culture, 158
    managing, 113, 189
    within people, 16
    in perceptions, 48
    relationships and business,
    56
    resistance to, 34, 127, 163,
    166
    speed of, 38
    unfreeze and refreeze
    model, 167, 167*ill*
    workloads, 136
change process, 102, 104, 106,
    107, 108, 109, 110

change-management, 29, 101, 127, 167

changing business environment, 6–13

charismatic leadership, 74

China Market Research, 126

Chrysler, 33, 143

Civilization and Its Discontents (Freud), 67, 67*n*

client focus, 34*ill*, 117, 117*ill*, 122, 144, 209

client information, sharing, 132

client problems, solving, 135, 172

client turnover, lower, 132

coaching, 155, 159*ill*, 161

Coffman, Curt, 130*n*, 224

cohesion, 87, 89, 94, 97, 103, 175, 179

cohesiveness, 80, 185

collaboration
  basis of, 72
  building foundation of, 29
  in business administration, 40
  culture of, 74
  effective relationships as foundation of, 149
  facilitation of, 75
  forming understanding, 162
  functions, 89
  mutual respect and, 27
  relationship issues and, 166
  replacing blame with, 139
  structure of interaction based on, 94

collaborative
  alliance, 100
  leaders, 185

Collins, Jim, 26, 34, 47, 224

commitment
  antiteam behavior and, 76
  assessing, 49
  to being customer focused, 131
  to being ethical, 125
  bringing to life, 169
  building foundation of, 29
  to community, 56
  delivering message of, 84
  embedding into organizational fabric, 52
  facilitation of, 75
  to learning and development, 68
  managing processes and, 189
  passion and, 209
  personal top down, 50
  providing framework for, 90
  to relationship and task, 94
  to social responsibility, 13
  to team, 93
  team lacking, 98
  to team meetings, 87
  to team values, 181

Committee of Sponsoring
Organizations, 125, 125*n*27
commonality, building, 84
communication
barriers to effective,
110–112
basis of, 72
building foundation of, 29
in building relationships,
125
conflict resolution and, 190
distinction between
dialogue and, 107
effective relationships
as foundation of, 149
engagement and, 25
facilitating, 88
facilitation, 75
forming understanding,
162
functions, 89
structure of interaction
based on, 94
community
building shared values and,
45
commitment to, 56
developing caring, 76
engagement in, 38
minded companies, 56, 168
community focus, of
corporations, 56, 180
Compaq Computer, 25

competition, 11, 14, 23,
24, 30, 39, 167
competitive advantage, 1, 32,
53, 121, 137, 151
competitiveness
applying knowledge to
increase, 38
future of, 19
individualism and, 109, 179
knowledge economy and,
24
of product or service to
end user, 40
quality movement and, 38
short-term earnings and,
23
society and, 62
sustainability and, 149
*The Complete Works of
Aristotle* (Barnes, ed.),
63, 63*n*
compliance
audits to ensure, 123
buy-in to, 145
statutory, 56
computer technology, applied
to tasks, 41
conceptual age, xv
conflict avoidance, 96, 99
conflict resolution, 111, 190
conflicts
autocratic leaders and, 89
cultural, 45
dissonance and, 69

internal, 86

interpersonal, 88

leaders feeling, 63

personality-based, 93

with stated values, 169

in team development,
91, 100

unresolved, 96

without aggression, 102

conscious leaders. *See also*
humanistic leaders

behavioral adjustments in,
184

change and, 103

communication *vs.*
dialogue with, 107

creating healthy teams, 75

as humanistic leaders, 68

manifests values, 62

mantra of, 66

relationship with team
members, 105, 110

team success and, 73

vs. unconscious leaders, 64

consensus building, 138

consolidation stage, 90–92, 96,
160, 176, 179, 181

constraints, theory of, 116

consumables, 19

continual improvement, 28, 33,
38, 149, 159

continual-improvement loop,
118

continuous improvement, 33,
143

control

developing, 145

effectiveness and, 18

framework for effective,
145

internal, 54, 55, 141,
145–146

locus of, 103

need for, 81

over responsibilities, 64

resolving issues of, 90

retaining ownership and,
139

of teams, 73–74

within teams, 87

in teams, 183

Controller's Handbook
(Shepherd), 200, 227

Cooper, K. M., 34, 224

core business

intelligence, 135

processes, 154

Core Model of Team
Development, 79–97

about, 81*ill*

amalgamation stage,
81, 89–90, 160, 177

consolidation stage, 81, 90,
90–92, 96, 160, 175, 181

deliberation stage, 81,
87–89, 92, 160, 175

evaluation stage, 81, 94,

95–97, 181
formation stage, 82–87,
92, 175
summation stage, 81,
92–95, 181
corporate social responsibility
(CSR), 12–13, 38, 56, 124
cost, reducing, 27
cost compliance, 162
cost-per-transaction basis, 154
costs
current, 19
cutting of, 23, 135
developing partnerships to
lower, 37
of external departments,
143
long-term approach to
viewing, 85, 109
managing IT, 144
reducing, 39–41, 39*ill*, 53
reducing poor quality, 32,
33
reducing supplier, 142
relationships and reducing,
38
viewing people as, 128
Courage to Love Yourself
(Parviainen), 190, 190*n*
Covey, Stephen, 14, 134, 188,
224
creativity
increasing, 72, 91

innovation and, 13, 15,
142, 149
CRM (Customer Relationship
Management), 132–133
Crosby, Phil, 33, 188–189
cross-cultural variation, 46
cross-functional representation
of roles, 87
cultural commitment,
long-term, 85
culture
of collaboration, 74
effective leadership
creating, 118
focus on, 128
cultures
building and sustaining,
113, 192, 195
change and, 114
clash of, 126, 167
collectivist, xiv
continual improvement, 28
cooperative and
collaborative, 2
positive team, 76
customer focused
commitment to being, 131
process of being, 209
Customer Relationship
Management (CRM),
132–133
customers
empathy with, 135
failing to involve key, 53

relationships between buyers, suppliers and, 40 relationships between clients and, 132 relationships between employees, suppliers and, 50 relationships between sellers and, 14

cynicism, 76, 99, 107

delegation
  of authority, 142
  of responsibility, 158
deliberation stage, 81, 87–89, 92, 160, 175
demands
  creating workforce, 18
  daily environmental, 179 new business, 181
  responding to difficult, 66
Deming, J. Edwards, 11, 32, 36–37, 117, 146, 188–189, 223, 224
The Deming Management Method (Walton), 228
democratic leaders, 89, 102
Descartes, 101
design
  development and, 137
  organizational, xvi

Design for Manufacturability. (Anderson), 27, 27*n*, 223
Desson, Stewart, 191
detachment
  dissonance and, 103
  rational emotional, 66
Deutsch, Helen, 97
dialogue
  communication and, 107
  encouraging, 100, 167
  internal, 61
dignity, 67, 81, 100, 110, 183
Dimensional Model of Human Behavior, 21*ill*, 184–185
Dimensional Selling (Buzzotta and Lefton), 224
direction
  focusing on clear, 120
  outcome expectations and, 119
  oversight and, 56
  positive developmental, 179
  team lacking, 98
disagreements
  addressing, 111
  attitudes toward, 67, 100, 108
  between board and leadership, 125
  tense, 88
Discovering the Soul of Service (Berry), 48, 223
disillusionment, 77, 85, 99

disobedience, 67

disorganization, leaders feeling, 63

dissonance, 62, 69–71, 99, 103

distance, emotional, 60

diversity, 180, 209

DMAIC (Define, Measure, Analyze, Improve, Control), 147

doing what makes sense, 209

dot com meltdown, 6, 145

easygoing leadership style, 185

EBA (emotional bank account), 14, 104, 105, 134

economy
industrial, 6, 23, 41
knowledge-based, 141
service sector of, 19–20
tangible and intangible, 6
twenty-first-century, 121

education, training and, 1, 2–3, 11, 35

Edvinsson, Leif, 8, 225

EFEM (European Foundation for Quality Management) criteria, 36*ill*, 116

effective leaders, 62, 72, 84, 89, 90, 106, 155, 190

effective leadership, 1, 10, 42, 118, 124, 152, 175, 194

effective organizations, 80, 132

effective presentations, 44

effective process management, 139

effective relationship building, 139

effective relationship management, 141

effective relationships, 9*ill*, 168

Effective Selling Through Psychology (Buzzotta, Lefton and Sherberg), 21*n*

effective strategic linkages, 166

effectiveness, planning for, 119–124

egocentric leaders, 66, 67, 134

egocentric thinking, 66

eight stages of psychological development, Erikson, 187, 187*ill*

either/or approach, 5

Elkington, John, 13

emotional bank account, 15, 105

emotional characteristics, of group, 185

emotional intelligence, 100, 110, 155, 179

emotional life of a person, 83, 105

emotional support, 91

emotionally secure *vs.* insecure leaders, 62–64, 72

emotions, 184, 185

The Empathic Civilization
(Rifkin), x, 185, 226
empathic listeners, 94
empathy, true, 67, 102, 110, 135
employees. *See also* people
   coddling, 127
   engagement of, 38
   engaging, 29, 140
   evaluation of, 52
   Fords relationship with,
   189
   infrastructure to support,
   150
   losing key, 13
   moment of truth for, 134
   partnering with, 10
   perception of, 49
   resistance of, 34
   teaching, 20
   town hall meetings with,
   85
   unmotivated, 142
empowerment, 25, 62, 72,
   90, 112
energy
   high-level, 178
   low-level, 100
   passive-aggressive behavior
   depleting, 111
   positive, 68, 86, 91
   sapping team, 109
energy-intensive existence, 186
engagement
   in change-management

initiative, 127
   communication and, 25
   effective, 155
   facilitating process of, 72
   loyalty and, 64
Enron, 145
environment
   adapting to external, xiv
   competitive, 165
   creating team
   environment, 86
   critical evaluation of work,
   109
   economic, 18–19
   low-trust, 107
   nonjudgmental and
   trusting, 72
   positive, 3, 188
   relational, 23–24
   sub values statements
   within working, 52
   transformed, 174
Erhard, Werner, 174
Erikson, Erick H., 187
Eriksons eight stages
   of psychological
   development, 187*ill*
ethics, 61, 98, 124–125, 190
Europe, 35–36, 44, 175
European Foundation for
   Quality Management, 116
European Foundation for
   Quality Management
   (EFEM)criteria, 36*ill*, 116

European mergers, 126
evaluation
    mentality, 96
    stage, 81, 94, 95–97
evolution
    of corporate social
    responsibility, 124
    of human race, 185
    of team development,
    162–163
The Evolution of Accountability
    (Shepherd), 201
excellence
    achieving, 36
    awards of, 35, 116
    framework for, 119
    models for, 8
    organizational, 141, 208
    people dimension in
    models for, 128
execution
    converting intent to, 27
    planning and, 149
    suppliers poor quality and,
    33
    task, 3, 17, 20–21, 23,
    25–26, 28, 37–38, 167
The Execution Premium
    (Kaplan and Norton), 34,
    225
executive function, of brain, 70
executives
    failure of mergers and, 127

    style of leadership, 186
    time spent by, 47
expectations
    alignment with stakeholder
    community, 121
    behavioral, 54, 56
    boards setting stage of, 119
    communicating in
    organization, 169
    in comprehensive
    orientation, 130
    core values and
    organizational leadership's,
    49
    discretionary, 58
    of leaders, general cultural,
    73
    leaders setting, 149
    outcome direction and, 119
    setting strategic, 120
    in task and relationship,
    123
    team meetings as clear, 87
    values reflecting
    community, 120
exploratory process, 71
external push, 85–86
externalism, 102

face-to-face service delivery,
    39, 136

facilitation, of set of Cs (team shamrock), 75–76

fact-based management, 210

failure

to achieve desired outcomes, 137

of M&As from cultural issues, 127

of M&As to address relationship management, 12

in making values real, 54

fast track approach, to implementation, 137, 137*ill*

FedEx, 20

feedback

leaders not open to, 70

in a learning organization, 117

listening skills and, 135

in performance management system, 115

in a sharing circle, 176

systems, developing, 50

Feigenbaum, A. V., 32

Field Theory in Social Science (Lewin), 108*n*, 226

financial performance, 13, 33, 123, 148

financial results

focusing on, 23

as outcomes, 123

financial statements, reliance on, 8

First, Break All the Rules (Buckingham and Coffman), 130, 130*n*

First Things First (Covey et al), 224

5 Percent Principle of Change, 103

followers, true, 109

followership, 64, 68, 109

Ford Motor Company, 33, 85*n*21, 189

formation stage, 81, 82–87, 92, 175

forming stage, 160*ill*

for-profit organizations, 6, 15, 31

foundation

of communication, 29

of continual improvement, 149, 159

for making change, 163

of organization, 4

of organizational activity, 119

of organizational behavior, 188

of organizational culture, 195

for relationships, 43–47

of self-motivation, 150

4P model, 26–28

fourteen points, Deming's, 11, 36, 37*ill*

framework
for commitment and action, 90
for competitive advantage, 15
for developing high-performing teams, 73
for developing management models for effectiveness, 116
for effective controls, 145
for excellence, TFM as, 119
for managing the unmanageable, 66
for organizational values, 194, 195*ill*
for training and help, 140
for understanding and improving leadership effectiveness, 192–194*ill*
for understanding team development, 79
for values-based leadership, 61
Frank, J. J., 32, 225
Freud, Sigmund, 67, 67*n*
Fromm, Erich, 179, 225
"Frontiers in group dynamics" (Lewin), 108
Fujimoto, Takahiro, 14, 122

General Motors (GM), 10–11, 15, 26–28, 33, 53, 143
getting on the bus, 130
Global Enterprise Value chart, 6, 6*ill*
global marketplace, 154
globalization, 30, 186
The Goal (Goldratt), 116, 116*ill*
Goethe, 69
going the extra mile, 209
Goldratt, Eliyahu M., 116, 116*ill*
Good to Great (Collins), 34
Goroff, Norman, 85, 178, 225
Gottman, John, 104
governance
board responsibility and, 125
compliance risk graphic, 58*ill*
corporate, 9, 54, 57, 145, 153
Governance, Accountability, and Sustainable Development (Shepherd), 9n, 153, 153*n*, 226
group development, models of, 79
group leaders, time spent by, 95
groups
achievements of, 195
attributes of, 185
as organizations, 187

successful relationships and, 187

value of success of, 185

GROWS action-planning approach, 220

Guardians, for team results, 178, 209

guides, to decisions and actions, 61

gung ho leaders, 63

gung-ho leaders, 101

gurus

management, 17

quality, 32, 36, 188

in quality movement, 11

values clarification, 49

Habeas Emotum, 105

Habits of Highly Effective People (Covey), 188, 224

Hammer, Michael, 189*n*38

Hand, J., 225

Harry, M., 33, 225

Harvey, David, xv

Havard, Alexandre, 62, 62*n*16, 225

haves and have nots, polarization of, 186

Hay Group, 126

Hewlett-Packard Company (HP), 25

hierarchy of needs, Maslows, 187

high task/high relationship managers, *vs.* high task/low relationship, 28, 28*ill*

high task/low relationship, *vs.* high task/high relationship managers, 28*ill*

historical values *vs.* book value, 155

holistic approach, 11, 21–22, 36, 65, 116, 183

holistic model, 35

holistic understanding, 109

Hollis, James, 60, 68

Honda, 26

Hope (Smyth), 227

hopefulness, sense of, 99

hopefulness, sense of, 89

Hoseus, Michael, 28, 28*n*

Hoshin Kanri, 21, 25

Hoshin Kanri (Akao), 21, 25, 223

HP (Hewlett-Packard Company), 25

human behavior

dimensional model of, 21, 184

as field of study, 182 reactive, 167

understanding, 22, 29

human beings

nature of, 102, 106, 186,

209
perception of others, 83
human capital, structural
capital creating, 129*ill*
human development, focusing
on, 85, 185
human dimension
developing, 191
effectiveness of task and,
188, 189
of performance
improvement, 5
task dimension and, 159
human engagement, 41, 189
human interaction,
effectiveness of, 53
human nature, 102, 106, 186,
209
human relationships, 12, 45
human soul, 190
human traits, values related
to, 65
humanistic leaders. *See
also* conscious leaders
description of, 67, 68
notion of power, 65
view of pseudo teams, 98
humanistic psychology
on needs of people, 182, 183
vs. Power Paradigm, 178
humanistic values, absence in
workplace of, 67
*Humanizing the Narcissistic
Style* (Johnson), 225

human-relationship
management, 42
human-resource management,
xvi, 41
humor, 68, 181

ICCS (Institute of
Citizen-Centered Service),
54, 54*ill*
implementation
in change process, 110
description of, 119
fast track approach to,
137–138, 137*ill*
of process, 108
in process management,
139–140
of quality systems
standards, 33
improvement
constant, 210
continual searching for,
195
continuous, 143
in cost, 41
cycles, 146
Dimensional Model
outcomes for team, 184
employee engagement in
driving, 38
measurable impact of, 170,
170*ill*

as measurement of
performance, 153

in morale, 103

in relationships,
measuring, 156

self-assessment program
for, 59

in tasks, 166

value chain management
and, 40

inclusion
lacking, 109

in teams, 183

India, xiv, 126

individualism
competitiveness and, 109

society and, 62

values of competitiveness
and, 179

individuals
great, teams of, 73

in Maslow hierarchy, 187

in organizations, 4

in past, 45

relationships and, 22

self-awareness as, 43

Industrial Revolution, 14

Information age, xv

Inglehart, Ronald, 46

Inglehart-Welzel Cultural Map
of the World, 46*ill*

initiatives
continuous improvement,
33

implementing new,
137–138

implementing quality,
21 improvement, 29, 33

supplier cost-reduction, 27

to use resources effectively,
32

innovate or die, xv

innovation
creativity and, 13, 15, 141,
149

as a measurement of
performance, 153

Institute of Citizen-Centered
Service (ICCS), 54, 136,
136*ill*

Institute of Management
Accountants (IMA), 224,
227

Insurance Day (magazine), on
M&A failures, 127

intangible, values, 8, 9, 13, 14,
128, 155

Intangible Assets (Head and
Lev), 225

Intangible Capital (Adams and
Oleksak), 8*n*, 223

Intangible Finance Tracker
2009 (Brand Finance), 7*ill*,
223

intangible intensity, increasing,
10

intangibles, 6, 7, 8–9, 12, 19,
131, 149, 155

integrity, 62

Intel, 25

Intelectual Capital (Stewart),
19, 19*n*, 227

Intellectual Capital
(Edvinsson), 8, 225

intellectual capital, sustaining,
129

interdepartmental
activities, 10
processes, 38, 138

internal controls and task/
relationship, 144

interpersonal
disconnection, 86
issues, 111
relationships, 14, 64, 176,
179

investments
in building relationships,
152
in emotional bank account,
15, 105
in human potential, 151
in teams, 80
in tools, 149

Iraq, 24

irony, 68

"Is/Is Not" tool, 50, 51, 133,
133*ill*, 169

ISO 9001 Quality Management
System, 134, 139, 140

ISO 10014, 33

ISO 14001, 124

I-Thou relationship, 64–65

James, William, 66

janitor, high-performing, 134

Japan, 20–21, 25–26, 28

Johnson, Sue, 91, 174, 225

Johnson & Johnson, 13, 13*n2*

joint venture, 38, 39, 43, 55,
124, 163–171

joint venture partners, 142, 164

journey, inner, of
self-discovery, 102

Jung, Carl, 63, 86, 93, 191

Juran, Joseph M., 32, 188–189

Juran's Quality Control
Handbook (Frank), 225

Kaplan, Robert S., 34, 152,
152*n*, 225

Ken, E, 226

key asset of organizations,
working relationships, 165

key drivers
for client satisfaction, 136
in ethical organizational
behavior, 125
of satisfaction, 54, 136

key employees, losing, 13

Kirchenbaum, H., 227

knowledge
  economy, 24, 53, 54, 140,
    144, 145
  management, 8, 149
  workers, xvi, 18
knowledgeable staff, 54, 136
knowledge-based
  organizations, 145
knowledge-based societies, 6,
    152

The Language of Change
  (Watzlawick), 228
leaders
  activities in developing
  organizational values, 50
  after summation stage, 93
  autocratic, 89
  building trust on teams, 71
  creating work
  environment, 188
  democratic, 89, 102
  developing atmosphere of
  openness and safety, 101
  developing empathy, 102
  education of, 1
  egocentric, 66, 67, 134
  emotionally secure *vs.*
  insecure, 62–64, 72
  financial aspects of job
  and, 189, 190
  focusing on tasks,

148 gung-ho, 63, 101
  identification with team,
    183
  influence on mood,
    183–184
  key aspect of following, 48
  maintaining sense of
  cohesion, 94
  moving from external
  push to internal pull, 86
  narcissistic, 62–65, 67, 122
  paying lip-service to
  values, 60
  role in amalgamation stage,
    89–90
  role in as-if teams, 97
  role in change process, 106,
    107
  role in consolidation stage,
    91
  role in deliberation stage,
    88
  role in evaluation stage,
    96–97
  role in formation stage, 83
  self-understanding
  assessment of, 179
  strength of organization
  and, 62
  supporting principles, 82
  tracking value of
  enterprise, 155
leaders role
  in building effective

relationships, 149

in Deliberation stage, 88

leadership

as art of managing the
unmanageable, 66

as base for applying
knowledge, 131

behavioral application of
values, 182–190

blind spots, 99

change and, 101–109,
108*ill*

character of, 62

dissonance and, 69–71

effective, 1, 10, 42, 118,
124, 152, 175

integration of values and,
60–62

love and, 178

and management matrix,
152*ill*

metrics linking back to,
155

operational, 125

organizational
theory and, 182–195

principle-centered, 103,
188, 224

reflective, 61

self-governance as highest
form of, 63

styles of, 185, 186

team effectiveness and,
71–74, 74*ill*

values-based, 61, 65, 69

values-based organization
and, 78

leadership development

individual, 171

paradigms of, 178

leadership effectiveness

improving, 192, 192–194*ill*

process of, 102

Leadership for Financial
Managers (seminar), 163

*Leadership Guide for
Healthcare Professionals*
(Stewart and Mazza), 227

leadership skills, 34, 130

*Leadership Through People
Skills* (Lefhon and
Buzzotta), 21*n*, 226

Leading at a Higher Level
(Ken), 226

The Lean Office (Collection),
224

learning, facilitating process
of, 72

learning organizations, 117,
140

Lefton, Robert Eugene, 21*n*,
111, 184, 224, 226

Leland, H., 227

Lev, Baruch, 8, 225

Lewin, K., 108, 108*n*, 167,
167*ill*, 226

Lewin theory of change model,
108, 108*ill*, 108*n*

Liker, Jeffrey, 21, 25–26, 25*n10*, 28, 28*n*, 29, 85*n23*, 226

linkages
  direct, 32
  effective strategic, 166
  encouraging, 84
  external, 149
  minimal, 54
  between tasks, 168, 169
  true, 132

listening skills, 135

long-term relationships, 27, 93

long-term strategic thinking, 26

Lopez, Ignacio, 10, 27

Lopez's supplier cost-reduction initiatives, 26–27

Love Paradigm *vs.* Power Paradigm, 178

loyalty, 14, 64, 90

Luft, Joseph, 105*n*, 226

Lumina Learning's Spark portrait, 191

Macdonald, John A., x

MacDuffie, John Paul, 14, 122

Magna, 10

Mahoney, F. X., 8, 226

Maisel, L. S., 224

Making it on your own, 109

management
  basis of, 147

control, 25, 161
  culture, changing, 158
  delegating responsibility away from, 140
  effective, 152
  effective relationship, 141
  fact-based, 210
  flavor of the month approach, 137
  gurus, 17
  implementation of quality systems standards, 33
  and leadership matrix, 152*ill*
  lean, 26, 32–33
  models, 35, 58, 153
  planning, 147
  quality, 11, 32, 116
  silo, 139
  statement of organizational vision, 121
  style, 18, 161
  teams, 80, 158, 163, 180, 181
  theories of, 47

management discussion and analysis (MD&A), 23

managers
  evaluating performance of, 27
  focusing on measuring tasks, 148
  as knowledge workers, 18
  metrics for, 155

people skills required by,
184

styles of leadership, 185

understanding
organizational culture, 128

working behind closed
doors, 104

managing by the numbers,
focusing on, 23

Mandela, Nelson, 101

manufacturers, 11, 19, 20

manufacturing, 18, 35, 99,
157–163

mapping business processes,
xiii

market value *vs.* book value, 7

Marlboro Man, 24, 186

Marx, Groucho, 82

Maslows hierarchy of needs,
187

matrix, 111*ill*, 152, 152*ill*

Mazza, C., 227

McKinsey and Company, 126,
130

measurable improvements, 3,
170, 170*ill*

measurements
financial, 8
intellectual capital, 129
multidimensional, 147
of organizational activity,
118
systems of, 147, 149
using, 151–156

measures
effective performance, 13
traditional core Jungian,
191

measuring, leadership
effectiveness, 153–156

meetings
to achieve success, 80
no time for, 127
punctual for, 69
purposeful and clear, 91
team, 82, 87, 164
town hall, 85

members. *See* team members

Mergers and acquisitions
(M&As), 12, 126, 127,
131–132, 167

Merrill, R. A., 224

Merrill, R. R., 224

metrics, developing leadership,
155–156

Middle East, xiv

Mielly, Michelle, xvi

MIL Standard, 33

misalignment, 49, 52

mission
aligning, 53
behavior and, 149
building organizational
culture using, 195
commitment to, 209
developing organizational,
54
mirroring corporate

direction, 146
outcomes and, 169
in relation to team
purpose, 177
shared, 132
sharing common values
and, 113
vision and, 118
mission statements, 57, 131
models
change management, 167
Core Model of Team
Development. *See*
Core Model of Team
Development Dimensional
Model of Human Behavior,
21*ill*, 184–185
4P model, 26–28
of group and team
development, 79
performance excellence,
35, 116
Plan, Do, Check, Act.
See Plan, Do, Check, Act
(PDCA) model power over,
64, 65
RP5 Management Model
of Excellence, 5, 208–209
Task-Relationship Model,
119–124, 120*ill*, 124–131,
130, 164. *See also* Plan, Do,
Check, Act (PDCA) model
team development, 81
theory of change model

(Lewin), 108, 108*ill*, 108*n*,
116
unfreeze, change, and
refreeze model, 167, 167*ill*
Vision, Reality, Action, and
Support (VRAS), 172
*Modernization, Cultural
Change and Democracy*
(Inglehart and Welzel), 46
Moller, Claus, 140
moments of truth, 134
Moments of Truth (Carlzon), 8,
140, 224
Monnet, John, x
moral vocabulary, 99
morale
improvement in, 103
poor, 77
Mortenson, Greg, 24, 24*n*, 226
motivation, 61, 62, 68, 70, 86,
99, 108, 129, 130
Myers-Briggs, 139

narcissism, 62–65, 67, 122
negative sentiment override
(NSO), 104
negotiation, facilitating process
of, 88
neuroscience, 70
*The New Organizational
Wealth* (Sveiby), 227
nine dot problem, 112*ill*, 221

nine-dot problems, 112

nonjudgmental, about, 79–82

norm, 77, 95, 96, 106, 176, 181

norming stage, 160, 160*ill*

North America, 24

Norton, David P., 34, 147, 152, 152*n*, 225

not for profit organizations, 6

not-for-profit organizations, 15, 17, 19, 22–23, 30, 35, 95, 133, 138, 154

NQI (Canadian Awards for Excellence) criteria, 36*ill*, 116

NSO (negative sentiment override), 104

Of Human Interaction (Luft), 105*n*, 226

Oleksak, Michael, 8, 8*n*

Ontario Municipal Employees Retirement System, 55

on-the-job training, 130

optimization, xv, 15, 116

organizational change, 11

organizational culture

changing, 10, 25

in creating competitive advantage, 12

developing values-based, 66

foundation of, 195

integration and, 113

perpetuating, 27

organizational effectiveness

building, 29, 114 core

components of, 123

delivering, 119

enhancing, 32

gaining competitive advantage through, 151

issues underlying, 115

model for basis of, 118

social theories implications for, 183

organizational mission

developing, 54

reviewing, 169

organizational models

development of, 8, 49

linking relationships to, 146

organizational performance, 2, 35

organizational planning, 114

organizational resources

in process management, 41

in task work, 32

waste in, 77

organizational success, 12, 109, 137, 192, 210

organizational success checklist, 192–194

organizational theory and leadership, 182–195

behavioral application

of values in leadership, 182–190
  call to action, 192–195
  history of, 182
  use of psychometric assessments, 190–191
organizational values
  factors in creating, 165
  guardian of, 209
  hiring aligning with, 130
  impact on, 6
  importance of, 188
  sustainability of, 125–126
organizational values framework, building, 47–59
  applying concept of "Is/Is Not," 50–51
  changes in organizations, 47–48
  codifying values, 49–50, 50*ill*
  compliance risk graphic, 58
  embedding commitment into organizational fabric, 52–54, 53*ill*
  having organizations "get it," 54–59
  starting process in, 48
organizational vision, 54, 121, 169, 209
organizations
  assessing, 36
  balanced, 135
  competitive, 132, 154
  conformity in, 109
  description of, 4, 17–18, 80, 187
  enhancing effectiveness, 150
  ethical, 125
  excellent, 148
  focusing on task, 152
  as groups, 187
  initiatives to enhance task, 137
  knowledge-based, 145
  leaders and strength of, 62
  lean, 131
  learning, 117, 140
  merging shared values, 126
  moving forward, 195
  not for profit, 6, 15, 17, 19, 22–23, 30, 35, 95, 133, 138, 154
  operations of, 114
  outcomes and value of, 22
  patient-centric, 180
  people as asset in, 129
  for-profit, 6, 15, 31
  relationship-based, 78
  service, 12, 53, 130, 138, 140, 167
  Tribal theory applied, 10
  values-based, 78
  working relationships, 165
orientation, 52, 92, 130

outcomes
  as competitive advantage, 5
  dissonant leaders and, 69
  effective, 65, 154, 210
  expected, 115
  financial results as, 123
  measurable, 184
  of narcissistic leaders, 64
  tangible, 53
  task execution and, 20
  value of organizations and,
  22
outsourcing, 13, 38, 40

Pakistan, 24
paradigm
  love, 178
  need for new, 14–16
  power, 178
  of self-centeredness, 65
  shift, 42
  teamwork, 81. *See also*
  Core Model of Team
  Development
paradox, 68, 101
partners
  engaging, 29
  outsourcing, 142
  people and, 26
  relationships with, 27
  selection of, 144

  suppliers and, 10, 142, 149
  treating consistently, 55
partnerships, 44, 124
Parviainen, Janice Mae, 190,
  190*n*
passion, 65, 209, 210
A Passion for Excellence
  (Peters), 8, 226
passive-aggressive manner, 96,
  109
paths, clear career, 164
patient-centric organizations,
  180
Patrick, St., 75, 136
Paul Tillich, 86
payback, 151, 152
payroll costs, 41
Peale, N. V., 223
people. *See also* employees
  as assets, 129–130
  buy in to organizational
  values, 52
  in change, 107
  dimension in models for
  excellence, 128
  as enablers of intangible
  value, 14
  focus and client focus,
  34*ill*, 117*ill*
  held to account, 68
  partners/suppliers and,
  142–144
  process dimension and,
  137–142

process framework, 140

skills, 184

working together, 132

perceptions

of change, 102

changes in leadership and, 48

employee, 49

fixed and unexamined, 98

performance

alignment in evaluations of, 131

attributes influencing, 185 business planning and, 123 excellence, 35, 36

management, effective, 115

performance management

basis for, 118

linkage to, 54

performance measurements

basis for systems of, 147

organizational, 152

performing stage, 160, 160*ill*

personal

development, 65

inadequacy, 77

relationships, 102, 122, 187

requirements, 61

personal transformations, process of, 102

personality profiling, 100

personality traits, 190

perspective

balanced, 73

changing, 168

of defined values, 61

ecological systems, 103 grandiose, 65

interpersonal, 75

operational, 51, 156

psychological, humanistic, 183

risk-management, 125

tools/task, 41

Peters, Tom, 8, 226

Peterson, Donald E., 85, 189, 189*n*37, 226

PFC (prefrontal cortex), 70

"*A Phenomenological Typology of Narcissism*" (Smyth), 227

philosophy, 100, 109

Pink, Daniel, xv

Plan, Do, Check, Act (PDCA) model, 114–119, 114*ill*, 118*ill*, 146, 148*ill*. See also Task-Relationship Model (TRM)

planning

to be effective, 149

for effectiveness, 119–124

linking results of, 158

management, 147

need for, 123

organizational, 114

process of, 66

Policy Deployment for Successful TQM, 25

Porter, Michael, 8

positions, operational leadership, 57

positive sentiment override (PSO), 104, 105

Powell, Colin, 47

Power, Bruce, 55, 56

power dynamics, 72

The Power of Ethical Management (Blanchard and Peale), 223

power over others, 111, 174

Power Paradigm, 64, 65, 178

Power Workers Union, 55, 56

Praxis, power of, 62, 62n17

prefrontal cortex (PFC), 70

preteam activity, 82

Principle of Change, 5 Percent, 103

principle-centered leadership, 103, 188, 224

Principle-Centered Leadership (Covey), 188, 224

principles
    application of, 182
    articulated, 61
    authoritarian, 179
    Demings fourteen, 11
    leaders supporting, 82
    leadership—one, 65
    productivity and, 99
    vs. values, 188

problem solving
    effective, 92, 101

facilitating process of, 72, 91

process, management, 17, 31, 32, 41, 139–140, 154, 189

process dimension, people and, 137–142

process-improvement teams, 20

Proctor and Gamble, 25

Project Management Institute, 31–32

project management tools, xiii

project-management techniques, effective, 32

pseudo teams, 98

PSO (positive sentiment override), 104, 105

psychological development, eight stages of, 187

psychometric assessment, 155, 158, 190–191

psychometrics, on-line, 179

Public Company Accounting Oversight Board, 125, 125n28

public sector leadership team, 171

QS 9000 automotive quality standard, 33

quality
    circles, 20

as a competitive advantage,
32

confidence in, 122

at Formation stage, 87

gurus, 32, 36, 188

ISO as framework for, 140

management, 11, 17, 32,
116

management initiatives, 20

management systems, 142

movement, 11, 32, 38

of team relationships, 101

validating production, 20

Quality Control Handbook
(Juran), 32

Quality Is Free (Crosby), 33

Quality Management System,
ISO 9001, 134, 139

questionnaires, 77

questions, in relation to
change, 101

Ratatouille (movie), 70, 70*n*

RCA (Resource Consumption
Analysis), 41

Reengineering Management
(Champy), 189

Reengineering the Corporation
(Hammer and Champy),
189, 189*n*38

refreeze model, unfreeze,
change and, 167, 167*ill*

Rein, Shaun, 126

relationship
commitment to team, 181

development, xv, 164

focus, 22

high task and high, 27

management, 12, 118, 141,
194

perspective, 110

in teams, 183

relationship, integration of task
and, 113–150

about, 113

being customer focused,
131–136

developing excellent
organizations, 148–150

human dimensions for,
124–131

internal controls, 144–146,
146*ill*

linking to results and
improvements, 146–148,
148*ill*

outside organization,
142–144

planning for effectiveness,
119–124

process dimension and
people, 137–142, 141*ill*

TRM model, 120*ill*

relationship-based
organizations, 78–112

applying Core Model.

See Core Model of Team Development

barriers to communication, 110–112

change and leadership, 101–109, 108*ill*

"as-if" teams, 97–101

matrix addressing disagreement, 111, 111*ill*

nine dot problem, 112, 112*ill*, 221

values-based organization, 78

relationships

high task and low, 27

in models for excellence, 146

shared values and, 43–47

Relin, D., 24, 226

requirements

capital investment, 51

compliance with, 32

interpersonal, 61, 82

task-relationship, 80

of team effectiveness, 73

understanding, of change process, 104

resistance to change, 34, 163

Resource Consumption Analysis (RCA), 41

responses

to change, 106, 110

defensive, 44

encouraging, 84

individually to change, 106

overemotional, 63

reactive, 97, 104

scripted, 135

responsibilities

corporate social, 12, 13, 38, 56, 124

delegating, 140

delegation of, 158

personal, 183

Rifkin, James, 226

Rifkin, Jeremy, x, 185, 226

risk, organizational control, 54, 141

risk management, 125, 144–145

RP5 Management Model of Excellence, 5, 208–209

Sarbanes-Oxley (SOX), 56, 125, 141, 145

Schuman, Robert, x

Search of Excellence (Peters), 8, 226

Second Sex (Beauvoir), xiii

self

absorption, 62

developing, 86

dignity of, 67

knowing, 169

sense of, 86, 97

team members sense of, 86
understanding of, 191
self-actualization, 67
self-assessment, 59
self-awareness, 43, 63, 158, 168
self-centeredness, 63, 65
self-concept, of team, 77
self-definition, in team
development, 86
self-development, 188
self-discovery, inner journey,
102
self-governance, 63
self-motivation, 150
self-perception, changing, 97
self-respect, 67
SEMA Group, 19
service delivery, 19, 31, 39, 136,
171
service economy, 141
service management, 48
service organizations, 12, 53,
130, 138, 140, 167
service workers, 133
shamrock, team, 75–76, 176
shared values
developing team, 84
merging organizations and,
126
organizational, 48
relationships and, 43–47
teams not founded on, 98
Shepherd, Nick
Controller's Handbook,
200, 227
The Evolution of
Accountability, 227
Governance,
Accountability, and
Sustainable Development,
9n, 153, 153n, 226
Values and Ethics, 200, 227
Sherberg, Manuel, 21n
Shewhart, Walter, 146
silos, 139, 149
Simon, S., 227
Simon, Sidney, 49
Six Sigma, 26, 33, 138
Six Sigma (Harry), 225
skills
job-related, 80
knowledge workers
analytical, xvi
listening, 135
people, 184
Smyth, Peter J.
"Hope," 227
"A Phenomenological
Typology of Narcissism,"
227
"Understanding Yourself
and Others" (Smyth), 96,
111, 172, 227
social agencies, growth of, 19
The Social Construction of
the Feeling of Personal
Inadequacy (Goroff), 225
social identity theory, 183

social psychology, on needs of
people, 182, 183
societal/cultural values, 45
societies, knowledge-based, 6,
152
Society of Energy
Professionals, 56
Socratic approach, 72
software systems, developing, 1
Souba, Wiley, 102
soul, 190
South America, 24
SOX (Sarbanes-Oxley), 56,
125, 141, 145
SPC (Statistical Process
Control), 20, 26
stages, of team development,
81, 160, 160*ill*
stakeholder relationship
building, 123
stakeholders
leaderships role with, 125,
165
organizational values and,
54
shareholders as, 121
standards, quality systems, 33
Statistical Process Control
(SPC), 20, 26
status quo, 77, 133, 209
Stewart, Thomas E., 8, 19*n*, 227
storming stage, 160, 160*ill*
Strengths, Weaknesses,
Opportunities, and

Threats (SWOT), 121, 122,
123–124*ill*
Stronach, Frank, 10
summation stage, 81, 92–95,
181
Sun Tzu, 99
suppliers
building relationships with,
27, 44
buyers collaborating with,
41
changing, 39
choosing, 20
failing to involve, 53
partners and, 10, 149
people and partners and,
142–144
poor quality by, 33
reducing, 37
relationships between
buyers, suppliers and, 40
relationships between
employees, customers and,
50
supply chain, 40, 41, 143
survival, xiv, 34, 68, 152
Sveiby, Karl, 8, 227
SW2C (So What? Who
Cares?), 29
SWOT (Strengths,
Weaknesses,
Opportunities, and
Threats), 121, 122, 123,
123–124*ill*

synchronous vibration, 108

synergy forms, 71

tangible assets, 8, 9*ill*, 14, 19, 20

tangible facilities, 18

tangible outcomes, 53

task

dimension, 29, 159

effectiveness, 17, 18, 37–38, 43, 100, 119, 160

execution, 3, 17, 20, 21, 23, 25–26, 28, 37–38, 167

high task/high relationship *vs.* high task/low relationship managers, 27, 28*ill*

orientation, xv

performance, 146

perspective, 110

task improvement, effective outcomes through, 154

task integration with relationship, 113–150

being customer focused, 131–136

developing excellent organizations, 148–150

human dimensions for, 124–131

internal controls, 144–146, 146*ill*

linking to results and improvements, 146–148, 148*ill*

outside organization, 142–144

planning for effectiveness, 119–124

process dimension and people, 137–142, 141*ill*

TRM model, 120*ill*

task-relationship, 21, 68, 98

Task-Relationship Model (TRM), 119–124, 120*ill*, 124–131, 164. *See also* Plan, Do, Check, Act (PDCA) model

tasks

commitment to team, 181 focusing on, 148

improvement in, 166

linkagen betveew, 168, 169

management focus on, 18

team

hierarchy, 88

identity, 71, 89, 91, 98

team cohesion, leader dominance and, 73

team development

commitment to, 84

conflict avoidance in, 96

Dimensional Model outcomes for, 184

evolution of, 162

facilitating process of, 72

model of, 81
models, 81
models of, 79
self-definition in, 86
team meetings in, 87
traditional stages of, 160
team effectiveness
duration of team and, 80
and leadership, 71–74,
74*ill* ownership and, 86
questionnaires, 77
team leaders
conscious, 100
effective, 71, 72, 79
role, 80, 82, 96
time spent by, 95
trained *vs.* untrained, 73
team leadership
development, 71
effective, 74, 100, 176
team learning, 71
team meetings, 82, 87, 164
team members
of closed-membership
teams, 80
commitment of, 75
embracing, 86
new, 82, 84, 92, 93
resistance to change, 166
respect for, 81, 82
sense of self, 86
of teams with prior
experience with each other,
83

team morale, 96
team process, 72, 79, 92
team self-definition, 86
team shamrock, 75–76, 176
team trust, 88
team vision statement, 84
teams
acting as individuals, 160
conscious, 68
describing their vision and
values, 85
description of effective, 80
developing, 86
developing values of, 84
dysfunctional, 96
effective, 75, 78, 159, 177
fully functioning, 90
high-functioning, 91
high-performing, 73, 79
not founded on shared, 98
pseudo, 98
purpose of, 76, 83, 88, 90,
95, 177
short-term, 80
synergistic, 90
transitioning, 95
underfunctioning, 77
teamwork, paradigm. *See*
Core Model of Team
Development
teamwork paradigm, 81
tested common sense, 184
theory
of change model, Lewin,

108, 108*ill*, 108*n*, 116
organizational, 182
social identity and group, 183
Tribal, 10
thinking outside the box, 112
Three Cups of Tea (Mortenson and Relin), 24, 226
360-degree feedback tools, 52, 100
timeliness, as driver of satisfaction, 136
time-space compression, xv
TMP (Toyota Management Principles), 25–26
TMS (Toyota Management System), 5, 21, 85
tools
    360-degree feedback, 52, 100
    ACT Assessment, 154, 171–172
    emotional-intelligence assessment, 191
    "Is/Is Not," 50, 51, 133, 169
Lumina Learning's Spark portrait, 191
psychometric assessment, 155, 158, 190–191
Toronto, 44, 54, 136
Total Quality Control (Feigenbaum), 32
Total Quality Management (TQM), 8, 20

town hall meetings, 85
Toyota, 14–15, 29, 53, 85, 121, 122, 143
Toyota, 15
Toyota Culture (Liker and Hoseus), 28, 28*n*, 85
Toyota Management Principles (TMP), 25–28
Toyota Management System (TMS), 5, 21, 85
The Toyota Way (Liker), 25, 85, 226
TQM (Total Quality Management), 8, 20
The TQM Trilogy (Mahoney), 8, 226
traditional buyer/supplier relationships, focus of, 44
traditional/old industrial economy, 41
training, education and, 1, 2–3, 11, 35
TransCanada Corporation, 55
transformations, process of personal, 102
Treadway Commission, 125*n*27
Tribal theory, 10
triple bottom line, 13, 13*n*3
TRM (Task-Relationship Model), 119–124, 120*ill*, 124–131, 130, 164. *See also* Plan, Do, Check, Act (PDCA) model
true followers, 109

trust
  building, 56
  creating, 14, 55, 144–146, 183
  creating safety, 91
  EFA and, 104
  evoking, 66
  loyalty and, 64
  work environments lacking, 109
trusting environment, nonjudgmental and, 72
Tyco, 145
Tylenol scandal, 13

ultimate concern, 86
ultimate supply chain, 143
Unassertive leaders, 185
uncertainties, 68, 72, 83, 109
unconscious leaders, 61, 64
"Under the Hood at Toyota's Recall" (Wharton Business School), 14, 14n, 122, 225
underfunctioning teams, 77
Understanding Organizational Culture, 128
"Understanding Yourself and Others" (Smyth), 96, 111, 172, 227
unfreeze, change, and refreeze model, 167, 167ill
unions, 18, 56

uniqueness
  cultural, 113
  individual, 107
United Kingdom (UK), 126
Unrecognized Intangible Assets (Shepherd), 165ill, 227
US Department of Defense, issues MIL Standard, 33

validation matrix, 125
value chains, 8, 40
value statements, sound-bite-sized, 50
value system, assessing individuals, 52
value-added partnerships, 44
values. See also vision and values
  attention to, 66
  awareness of, 82
  behavior and, 49, 168
  building, 47
  conscious leader manifests, 62
  defining set of, 166
  developing team, 84
  driving behavior, 118
  ethics and, 124–125
  intangible, 8, 9, 13–14, 128, 155
  integrity and, 62
  internalization of, 61
  leadership and integration of, 60

merging organizations and
shared, 126
organizational. *See*
organizational values
paying lip service to, 50
vs. principles, 188
rational thinking, as guided
by, 66
reflecting expectations of
the community, 120
related to human traits, 65
in relation to team
purpose, 177
relationships and shared,
43–47
sharing common mission
and, 113
societal/cultural, 45
sustainability of
organizational, 125–126
teams not founded on
shared, 98
Values and Ethics (Shepherd),
227
values clarification guru, 49
values clarification gurus, 49
Values Clarification (Simon,
Kirchenbaum, and Leland),
227
values statements, 13, 47,
51–52, 56, 57, 131
values-based leaders, 65–68
values-based leadership, 61,
65, 69

values-based management, 43
values-based organizations, 78
values-clarification process, 61
variation, cross-cultural, 46
Virtuous Leadership (Harvard),
62, 62n16, 225
vision
aligning, 53
developing organizational,
54
mission and, 118
outcomes and, 169
without reality, 121
Vision, Reality, Action, and
Support (VRAS), 172–173,
180
vision and values
building organizational
culture using, 195
commitment to, 209
importance of, 71, 84, 85,
90
internalizing, 109
in relation to team
purpose, 177
statements of, 57, 131
vision statement, team, 84
Vonnegut, Kurt, 98
VRAS (Vision, Reality, Action,
and Support), 172–173,
180

Walton, M, 11, 228

Watzlawick, F., 228

Watzlawick, Paul, 106, 228

Weiss, Richard, 104

Welzel, Christian, 46

Wharton Business School, "Under the Hood at Toyota's Recall," 14, 14*n*, 122, 225

Whitewater affairs, 144

Whitmore, John, 71

A Whole New New Mind (Pink), xv

WIIFM (What's In It For Me), 29

win/lose strategy, 133, 138, 143–144, 186

win/win strategy, 143, 144, 186

World Values Surveys, 46, 46*ill*, 46*n*

Wyman, Oliver, 127

Xerox, 25

zero defects, 32, 154

zero waste, 26, 131